Writings
from the
Handy Colony

2-03

LOCAL EDITOR

Edited by

HELEN HOWE, DON SACKRIDER, AND GEORGE HENDRICK

Introduction by
JOHN BOWERS

Afterword by
JUDITH EVERSON AND J. MICHAEL LENNON

Tales Press
Urbana, Illinois

First Edition, 2001 by Tales Press, Urbana, Illinois

*Cover illustration: Lowney Handy photo taken at the swimming hole on the grounds of the
Handy Writers' Colony in Marshall, Illinois. Courtesy of the Handy Colony Collection,
Archives/Special Collection, University of Illinois at Springfield. Background photo by Ray
Elliott of the one-time Harry and Lowney Handy home in Robinson, Illinois, James Jones
lived with the Handys in the early days of the Colony and wrote much of From Here to
Eternity.*
Cover design by Carlton Bruett.

Library of Congress Cataloging-in-Publication Data

Writings from the Handy Colony / edited by Helen Howe, Don Sackrider,
George Hendrick ; introduction by John Bowers ; afterword by Judith
Everson and J. Michael Lennon.-- 1st ed.
    p. cm.
  ISBN 0-9641423-6-8
  1. American literature--Illinois--Marshall. 2. Handy, Lowney Turner--
Correspondence. 3. American literature--20th century. 4. Handy Writers'
Colony. I. Howe, Helen, 1927- II. Sackrider, Don. III. Hendrick, George.
IV. Handy Writers' Colony.
  PS572.M37 W75 2001
  810.8'09773515'09045--dc21

                                            2001004670

CONTENTS

PREFACE

The Handy Writers' Colony existed on an informal basis from 1943 to 1951, when it was incorporated. It continued until 1964, when Lowney Handy, the founder, died. This unique colony was headed by a non-conformist, a New Ager in Mid-America. She was a compelling conversationalist. She was quixotic and unpredictable. She was never to publish in her lifetime, but she turned herself into a perceptive editor. She believed in her students and made great efforts to ensure their success.

Lowney Turner Handy, wife of Harry Handy, an executive of the Ohio Oil Company in Robinson, Illinois, met a young, troubled James Jones in 1943. He had been wounded on Guadalcanal and, while recovering in a hospital in Tennessee, would go AWOL and return to Robinson, his hometown. Jones, deeply disturbed, wanted to be a writer, and Lowney immediately recognized his talent and became his literary guide, his tutor, his lover. She helped him get a discharge from the Army and moved him into the Handy home. Harry Handy supported Jones for years while he learned the art and craft of writing.

To escape the harsh Illinois winters, Lowney would take Jones to Florida for a few months. Jones at first worked on a novel, *They Shall Inherit the Laughter*, which he abandoned after several revisions. He then turned to writing *From Here to Eternity*, published in 1951. Lowney, in the meantime, began to recruit other students: Don Sackrider, Charlie Dawes Myers, Willard Lindsay. Harry gave her four hundred dollars a month to support the writing group. During her lifetime, Don remembers, Lowney received 10 percent of the royalties from both *Eternity* and *Some Came Running*. She also received 10 percent of some other Colony book royalties, and most of these funds went into support of the writers.

Lowney had begun developing her own plan for the teaching of creative writing. She had beginning students copy all or parts of novels or stories by John Dos Passos, Thomas Wolfe, F. Scott Fitzgerald, William Faulkner, John Steinbeck, Ernest Hemingway, and others before the students could begin their own work.

At first, the unofficial writing group operated out of the Handy home in Robinson and in winters traveled to Arizona, New Mexico, and California, as well as the more familiar Florida. In the summer of 1950, Lowney began a more formal colony in Marshall, Illinois, just north of Robinson. The site was a five-acre cow pasture belonging to Harry's mother. Over time a few buildings were in place: a ramada,* Lowney's cottage, Harry's cottage, barracks. Some students lived in tents or trailers. By 1952 twenty-two students were in residence, completely supported by the Handys and Jones. Lowney was the warden of the Colony, and the students (except Jones) lived on a strict schedule: up early, a light breakfast, followed by a morning of copying or working on their own creative work; lunch; an afternoon of working on the grounds (laying of brick walkways, building a swimming pool) and sports; dinner; early lights out. No liquor. Students were warned not to talk to anyone except Lowney about their own writings. The Colony buildings were not winterized, and the Colony did not operate in Marshall during the winter. Lowney would take a few students to a warmer state, a few might stay with Harry's mother, and others took temporary jobs.

Lowney often chose renegades and castaways as students, believing she could help them turn their harsh life experiences into fiction. She generally disliked working with women students, but a few, including Jones' sister, Mary Ann, were Colonists. She had many successes with the seventy or so students with whom she worked. At least twelve published novels and many stories were written at the Colony. Jones finished *Some Came Running* before he left the Colony.

---

*The word "ramada" intrigued Lowney, Harry and Jim. Originally it meant a simple shelter, but on the Colony grounds it was deluxe and large, partly screened and partly fully enclosed. There was a Bedford stone fireplace with bookshelves on each side, a large fully enclosed kitchen, and a carport and dark room for Jim.

James Jones married Gloria Mosolino in 1957, and they returned to Jones' home just outside the Colony grounds. Even though Jones did not tell his wife about his romantic relationship with Lowney, there was tension between the two women and finally Lowney made a violent attack on Gloria. The Joneses left Marshall and Illinois. Jones finally did confess to his bride his emotional entanglement with Lowney. Except for the royalties Lowney received from *Eternity* and *Some Came Running*, his support of the Colony stopped, but Lowney was able to keep it going for several more years. To the very end of her life she went on attempting to help her students.

We [George Hendrick, Helen Howe, and Don Sackrider] recently published *James Jones and the Handy Writers' Colony* [Southern Illinois University Press, 2001], an informal history of that unusual gathering of Lowney's students. During the course of our research we uncovered several unpublished writings connected with the Colony and have chosen several of them for this volume: a strong story by Lowney herself, sections from Harry Handy's novel, portions of Mary Ann Jones' novel, stories by Don Sackrider, a story by John Bowers, and a play about the Colony by Jon Shirota, the last student there. These previously unpublished selections provide readers with important new information about the Colony and some of its writers.

—H.H., D.S., G.H.

INTRODUCTION

We, of course, were never allowed to see each other's work at the Handy Colony. I even felt a little guilty seeing it in print, as when Jerry Tschappat's and Sonny Daly's books came out a short time after I left. A little strange, you might think. You don't know the half of it. The Handy Colony was as far away from Yaddo and MacDowell as the night the day. It was more like—shall I dare say it?—a cult rather than a learning center for the fashioning of prose. At its center was one powerful woman. She drew people to her in a messianic way. She left you never the same again. Her name was Lowney Handy.

Jon Shirota recounts here his sending a manuscript to Lowney in high innocent optimism, seeking admission, and its coming back like a rifle shot with "Shit" written on it. This was not unusual. It was Standard Operating Procedure. You were brought down and then you were lifted up, thinking absolutely differently about everything in the process.

Going back and reading these works from the Colony is strange for me. They evoke so much. "V for Victory," by Lowney herself (how weird to see work from someone who used to mark yours up and down!) recreates the atmosphere of WWII and slightly beyond. Vets are returning, a new world is opening up, the old order is about to be brought down. It is not in her voice—you have to go to her letters, some included here, for that, and even there you won't get the full pungent flavor—but it does capture that period and her role in it. Disturbed Vets were returning to small towns that didn't know what to do with them. (James Jones was one in real life.) The narrative has an unfinished quality and it's a little hard to follow, but if you knew her, you get the drift. There's Minnie, who kicks up her heels, has a lover, was "a dictator in the social whirl." There is the older Alfred, a paragon of understanding and patience, and white-haired Jacob, a poor vindictive devil who's been cuckolded. We place a lot of emphasis today on finding one's own voice. It's too bad hers seems filtered through Thomas Uzzell's *The Technique of the Novel* or some such tract. It's too formal and writerly for the raucous, explosive Lowney that I knew. She had a lot to say and had, pardon the expression, the balls to say it. If she had thrown off constraints and convention the way she urged us to, she might have concocted a masterpiece.

Helen Howe points out the gentle side of Harry Handy, how he had a talent for description, the ability to find the telling detail that men generally miss in trying to paint a picture. He was certainly not effeminate, but this quality shows a feminine side to him. In the excerpt from his novel his leading character is no monk and has flings with several women around a place called French Lick. Harry was a decent and deceptively conventional man. For all I know, he could have been the wildest of us all. He was hard to know because Lowney was the conduit to all knowledge about him, and Harry himself was generally potted and incoherent after the sun went down. Lowney did love him. The passion had gone out of the marriage by the time the Colony came along, but a deep bond remained between them.

For us minions, for us scribblers and strivers, it was assumed that we were beyond love; we were supposed to be beyond the complexities of family, a mother's concern, and the trappings of ordinary human life. I don't know exactly who cooked this all up in Lowney's brain, and it may be all right for a writer if taken with a grain of salt, but if you follow it to the letter, you are in danger of going cuckoo and losing all moorings. It left me shell-shocked. I had loved love right up until the day I walked into the Handy Colony. I left without the ability to fall in love again. So I was moved by my good friend Don Sackrider's story, "Ode to the West," in which Ellen says, "... a woman lives for someone [who] loves and needs her. If she doesn't feel really wanted, not needed, the flame inside goes out."

She leaves her lover Arch, who is devoted to music and Stan Kenton, the way we at the Colony were to writing and James Jones.

Sackrider has Ellen say, "... if there is a God to replace the Christianity our generation's lost, it won't be Kenton." Amen.

I wish I could have read "Ode to the West" at the Colony. I was suffering the pangs of thwarted love then myself but had no one to talk to about it or to admit how deeply and devastatingly I hurt. Lowney would have told me—had told me, time after time—that women just wanted to fill their wombs, have babies, and all guys were suckers to fall for their lines and artifice. That was it. The continuation of the race or the purpose of life was never brought up. You didn't get to talk about much of anything, let alone your real deep feelings, at the Colony. It was more Victorian than modern in that regard, despite the openness with which we described bodily functions at the dining table. There were deep feelings raging there, but the reality of them was sealed. There was the relationship between Lowney and Jim; then there was Lowney and Harry, then Lowney, Jim, and Harry. A lot was going on but only the tip of the iceberg showed. I wonder how much they expressed to themselves, or among themselves, of their real deep feelings. They were all too human for all their guardedness, though. A minute or two around them told you so. I know that for all her cussing and ranting and raving, Lowney was vulnerable and as sensitive as an open wound. She could be devastated by the slightest gesture of disapproval. Thus, she kept those who might disapprove of her as far away as possible-by cunning or sometimes by heaving a brick.

I never met Mary Ann, Jim's sister. She died in a convulsion the day before I arrived. Her manuscript is sketchy and unformed but shows inchoate feeling. So much work at the Colony, from the representative pieces here, were about repressed feelings and those (parents, society?) that had injured and forced those feelings to be locked up. Lowney obviously got through to Mary Ann. The character Olga Feathers in Mary Ann's *The Third Time You Killed Me* seems to be a stand-in for Lowney. Martha June [a stand-in for Mary Ann] replies hotly to her controlling aunt when accused of being changed by Olga Feathers. *"She didn't change me. She only taught me."* [Italics mine.]

Helen Howe's insight into Burroughs Mitchell's critique of Lowney's novel, *But Answer Came There None*, that it could equally be applied to Harry's work is right on the money. Finally, in both their work you end up not caring about the characters. The reason is that the situations lack a human concern that works toward a denouement. I will go a step further and say that much Colony material that I've now seen lacks a sense of story. There is no universal human situation where the characters are working out their conflicts and dilemmas in a way that makes us want to turn the page. There are fine sketches, great dialogue, interesting characters presented—but no stories about people we identify with, love or hate, and read on to find what happens to them. There was one exception at the Colony, and his work is not included here. This is James Jones. His technique might change from *Eternity* through *Whistle,* but that marvelous sense of story was always there, his ability to make us care. He had God-given talent. I think possibly Lowney knew somewhere within her that talent was important. It was an elusive quality, though, that cannot be taught, even by someone as strongwilled as she. It might have caused some of her rages against us neophytes.

It is fitting indeed that Jon Shirota's play, *The Last Retreat*, should conclude this collection. He was the last survivor, someone left stranded on that Mount Everest we had all, one time or another, been trying to climb. Our trail maps did not include Chekhov, Joyce, and certainly not James, Henry. We never studied real history or Shakespeare, or the essays of Macaulay or Cyril Connelly. If you said Bloomsbury, we would have thought you were ordering ice cream. We didn't know what we were getting into. All we knew was that someone pointed out a high reach, some great distant spot covered by clouds, and tried to get us there past all endurance, past all reason. Some failed at base camp. Some got up part way. Some had to be carried down. But what a sight, that top of Everest! What a guide we had!

—*John Bowers*

An Editor's Note

I met John Bowers many years after our time together in the Handy Colony, and the first thing I did was confront him with what I thought was an unfair portrayal of the founders, Lowney and Harry Handy and James Jones in *The Colony*. Even though I found much truth in the book, I found it to be more of a caricature of the people involved. John did say that he had had to find a style and point of view which would make an entertaining story, and I had to admit it was entertaining—if you were not on the inside.

Later, when I reread John's introduction to the Handy Colony papers, which are stored at what is now the University of Illinois at Springfield, I found he had a mature and overall excellent analysis of the Handy Colony. Based on this, I suggested John as a good candidate to write the introduction for this book, and he did. When I read this introduction, I felt it was biased and have written a rejoinder.

I knew the principals, Lowney, Harry, and Jim, over a longer period of time than John, and I knew Lowney particularly was a many-faceted person. Jones had used many of those facets as a basis for characters in his novels. Lowney served as the basis for Karen in From Here To Eternity, Gwen in *Some Came Running*, and as the jealous lover in *Go To the Widowmaker*. I felt the *Widowmaker* character Carol Abernathy was unfair to Lowney and confronted Jones in Paris when we met after many years. Jones admitted that he probably should also have shown Lowney as she was when she was younger. When Jones said the word "Lowney" and not the name of the character in our conversation, I felt it was admission that he had drawn the character from Lowney. And most of us who knew him felt he was grandstanding for his wife Gloria in the novel.

If Harry Handy was an alcoholic, as John suggests, it did not affect his fine intellect or his commitment to Lowney and the Colony.

Bowers has said there were no books produced at the Colony that were real page-turners, except for Jones'. I disagree with that. There were several. Among them were Tom Chamales' *Never So Few*, Jere Peacock's *Valhalla* and Jon Shirota's *Lucky Come Hawaii*. Bowers' own book, *Stonewall Jackson: Portrait of a Soldier*, while not written at the Colony, was a fine page-turner. To continue the tradition, the ghosts of Lowney, Harry and Jim moved the members of the James Jones Literary Society to establish a James Jones First Novel Fellowship for an unpublished novel. Many of those recipients have published fine books.

—*Don Sackrider*

LOWNEY HANDY

Those of us who knew Lowney and Harry Handy and James Jones can easily see how this story grew from a visit by Jones and the Handys to the local Elks. Jones was the returning war veteran.

When I met the Handys and Jones in 1947, I was allowed to read Lowney's novel-in-progress and Jim's unpublished novel, They Shall Inherit the Laughter, *along with Jim's just begun* From Here to Eternity *and Jim's drawer of five unpublished stories. I do not remember seeing any stories by Lowney. To me, this story is like finding unpublished works by Mark Twain or Hemingway.*

The story turned up while I was going through a group of Lowney's letters for this book. Very likely, Lowney gave it to me when she stayed with me in 1963. It is unlike her novel, which had a soap box character preaching philosophy and religion. It is closer to poetry than prose. And, to me, it is like hearing from the other side.

—*Don Sackrider*

V FOR VICTORY

By Lowney Handy

"It wouldn't have been so bad if it hadn't been a beer sign." Herman's plump lips pouted his indignation.

"Lucky it didn't break." Dick's effort to appease Alfred was hampered by his desire to play along with the other two members of the committee.

"With the war, however, and everything ..." Dick was terribly proud of having been selected to the Board of Trustees, and, like Jacob and Herman, he was well aware of the great honor. His talents were unusual, for seldom was a newcomer so highly flattered; not only that but he was much younger. His rich voice dropped away into silence as he turned soulful bed-room eyes on the other three.

"That's it exactly. People are fully cognizant of the tremendous seriousness of the war. Now, if it had been some sort of cheap beer sign." Herman's lips were a congested near-purple and quivering with the pent-up feelings of his patriotism.

"But," Alfred began gravely, "that's really the whole point. Too many Civilians *just* don't realize. They take something symbolic like a blue neon sign and substitute that as of more importance than men's lives. After all, it's lost legs, not an electric neon sign that's important."

Jacob stirred restlessly. Alfred went on so, almost like a record. Jacob hoped he wouldn't have to enter the argument just yet. Over a long period of years, his silences had been acknowledged as subtlety. If you didn't say a thing, you didn't have to unsay it. Sooner or later, some rash person would make all the necessary speeches. Then, too, he was chairman of the board, and the final decorous summing up would be his. His word would be the final ultimatum. He was quietly pleased that Herman was keeping Alfred down. And Dick, too. He had been right about the youngster. Things surely were bad enough without older men of the community favoring the disgruntled soldiers and encouraging their wildness. Drunken troublemakers.

Alfred was still holding the floor. "The Civilians don't seem to realize how the soldiers feel. They don't understand their bitterness. These boys coming home, wounded, with months in the hospital, are still not adjusted. Really, they are still sort of punch-drunk."

Jacob had to admit he had never liked soldiers. And now all their talk about running things to suit themselves when they got home and organized. Soldiers. Jacob knew all there was to know about the breed. He could tell plenty if it were his policy to talk. It was scandalous some of the things the big, hulking young men would do to evade their country's call. He knew all there was needed to know to understand them. Hadn't he donated his services free to the Draft Board? He knew them all, they couldn't fool him, knew their parents before them. Working with them all day was depressing. He had told his wife there was something nauseating in the smell of soldiers. A strong, rancid odor always hung in their clothes. He was getting tired of Alfred's persistence.

"Really," Alfred was saying, "we don't any of us care much what happens to the boys. That is, unless they happen to be our own immediate family. And they know we don't care, too. Civilians are too smug. We only have an interest in our own lives, our own lucrative business affairs. It's this lack of understanding that makes the soldier bitter. They say we only care about making money."

"It's about time some of them acquired more respect for making money." Herman refused to meet Alfred's penetrating gaze. Heavy brown lids shut out the sudden glitter that any reference to money always brought to his eyes. Money was an obsession with him. Profits were his chief interest. Even when meeting a stranger, in no time, he would be figuring on the back of an old envelope his earning for that week, month, and year with detailed explanations. Alfred wondered if some terrible humiliation or deprivation had occurred in Herman's youth to have shut almost everything else out of his life.

"As members of the Board of Trustees," Herman continued, "it is imperative that we keep in mind that our principal duty is to the Club, the protection of its property and its continued welfare."

Alfred was curious as to what line of smooth palaver Herman would have ready for the returning soldiers when they became his future market. Would he slap them heartily on the back? And would they be impressed with this evidence of his liking? Would he, as always before, weave a kind of hypnotic spell with his sales platitudes and sign them on the dotted line?

"Of course, the Club must look after its property." Alfred's monotonous voice had a slow, sad undertone. "But the sign was not broken. I'm sure vagrancy wasn't intended. And banishing the boy from the Club is rather severe, don't you think? It was a gesture on his part, and no harm done. Tossing a handful of powdered coal was a sort of bitter mirth. You see, the soldiers feel that Fate has dealt them a lousy hand." Albert turned to Dick, sensing that possibly he was the least set of the three.

"It could easily have been you, Dick. You're young. Still of draft age. Jack is about your age. He's lost his leg, lost his business through being in the Army. Try putting yourself in his place. He feels he's lost everything: all his friends, that nobody cares. If the Club withholds their leniency, it looks as though he's about right."

Jacob was about ready to go home. There was a quite noticeable resemblance, he thought, between Alfred and the tenacious hanging on of Skip, his English bulldog. Alfred had the same determined clamp in his chin.

"Jack's spent months in the hospital. It takes time to rehabilitate. Maybe all of it doesn't need to be done by the soldier. Maybe the Civilian needs rehabilitating, too." Alfred turned to all three of them, noting Jacob's glance at his watch. Jacob, the old male hating the young. What was that pool room story? The saying, that as soon as Jacob spotted a big, husky young man he couldn't get him out of town fast enough. "I hope this committee will reconsider," Alfred said earnestly. "Try to understand, be more lenient. And you'll vote to change your decision."

He looked at Jacob, noting the sly wandering of his eyes, his snow-white hair, and thought that the years of Jacob's cuckoldry had left their mark. Knowing that your wife had a lover made you like Jacob. Funny thing what pride could do to a man. Of course, today probably would make a difference, but back in the mauve age, when Jacob's wife was young and fast, as they said then, the town's ostracism of Winnie had left its mark on Jacob. She probably hadn't really cared, for she didn't like women, anyway. Then, too, she had her lover over a long period of years to more than compensate; and when she had a desire for feminine gossip, there were hours to be spent in the selection of a dress, or with the hair-dresser, or with any of the wives of the tradespeople. They had time for her. And she had had the secret pleasure of degrading them with her money. Forcing them to suavely meet the situation, although there might have been a mild tincture of disrespect, something of the same attitude they would have had in serving big madam Sophie, still they couldn't refuse to visit. And now with the changing times, old enemies gone, dead or moved away, and Jacob's increasing wealth and his philanthropies, his serving on all the important boards, she was now a dictator in the social whirl.

Alfred was ready to go home, too. They all were tired. He couldn't think of anything more to say. Jacob was getting to his feet stiffly and ponderously.

"It would seem to me, gentlemen, that this subject has been exhausted and there isn't much more left to say. We have gone through it before, the entire happening from beginning to end, and made a decision. There has been nothing new brought up tonight, as I see it, to alter the original conclusion. For the Club's good, there was no other policy left the Board. We have had a number of complaints about this boy. One thing not brought up here tonight was an objection to the sort of coarse language he used. Jack made himself extremely objectionable, completely ignoring the presence of ladies within the Club. Gentlemen, no rehabilitating, I am sure, will correct his blackguarding, his sullen manner. Furthermore, you will concede that there is no reason to subject ourselves to coarseness, nor insults to our wives. I object, in particular, to the crude remark he made when throwing the coal. In an exceptionally loud voice, and one you will admit is especially carrying, he said, since there was nothing else to throw, that all the cows inside the Grill Room were house broke."

The committee members put on their coats and hats and left the room. They turned up the street toward town without looking back. And Alfred climbed alone up the stairs to the street door. The blue neon light emphasized the pugnacious set of his face. He wasn't whipped yet. He'd do something else. Just what, he didn't know. He laughed wryly.

Alfred had gone a couple of blocks before he realized his laughter was loud and strong.

[This story is not dated, but probably belongs to the period of 1945 when Jones was writing They Shall Inherit the Laughter, *which contains a similar scene, but told from the point-of-view of the young man. Tinks Howe remembers Lowney's work on a novel,* From Riches to Bitches, *which apparently contained similar themes. —*EDS.*]*

EXTRACTS FROM
LOWNEY HANDY ON THE HANDY COLONY

November 7, 1952

CONFIDENTIAL—as this material has been sold to a well known magazine for publication.

Writers come and go at the Colony. Some have been called by

Navy and Army, some go to school, some decide the climate is bad and take a year away. Some longer or shorter.

I always try to keep the barracks filled, that means 5 students to each barracks—of which there are two. I have had more than that often. This spring for six weeks or more there were four tents in operation. There is an old dilapidated trailer with a room added that serves as a magazine library and bed storage but can be put to use if necessary. Besides that we have a small good trailer with bathroom, that was occupied by James Jones' sister Mary Ann until her death in June.... I have a guest cabin that I try to keep empty for guests but often put a writer in there in a pinch. Besides this there is James Jones' Spartan Trailer that no one occupies but himself.

After we close camp—which is basically from frost to frost but we have stayed this year until November 8th, with one bathhouse heated and electric heaters in the barracks, only four have remained since first of October. These four who are the ones that are closest to publication—two will go with us (supported by gift funds) to winter quarters. Two will remain with my husband's mother, and supported by Harry E. Handy. This was the policy followed last year....

In choosing the writers since Jones' success, and even prior to that, I have been approached by writers who have learned of the work we are doing. Some have been sent by friends and others brought into the Colony by members. However, since the publicity of the camp and Jones' novel I am swamped with applicants. In order to save myself work and to weed out only those who really and sincerely desire to make writing a lifelong work I have devised a series of studies. There is a good deal of plain unromantic labor involved and many do not complete this program, If they do all that I require, mailing in to me the things they have finished, then and then only, are they ready for an interview. Usually I choose in the fall the ones who can come in with me the following spring....

The private residence and home of Mr. and Mrs. Harry E. Handy (Lowney T. Handy) is Robinson, Illinois—202 West Mulberry. Mr. Harry E. Handy is superintendent of the Ohio Oil Refinery located in Robinson. Mrs. Handy spends part of her time at home but a greater part is spent at the Colony in a small cabin, re-converted from a garage moved to the grounds. Lowney Handy not only is in charge of the Colony with all problems that come up with the personal relations. Seeing, that things go smoothly, in charge of construction going on the job. Doing the buying of food (sometimes as many as 25 to be served meals) and doing the cooking—WITH NO HELP EXCEPT THE STUDENTS, who take turns two at a time helping on KP.

Part of the MATURING or education of the writer includes learning how to live to a system, how to cook and take care of himself and any jobs that come up such as carpentering, bricklaying, concrete pouring, construction work.... The writer spends only six hours a day writing. Any more tends to make the student less healthy than Mrs. Handy thinks best....

The Colony is supported by three people only. JAMES JONES, AUTHOR OF *FROM HERE TO ETERNITY*. HARRY E. HANDY, SUPERINTENDENT OHIO OIL REFINERY, ROBINSON—and this year by Mrs. Lowney T. Handy, who earned 10% from Jones' novel as teacher—AND RE-INVESTED IT ALL BACK INTO THE COLONY. Within two months of receiving earned income the total of cash received had been spent on the group here. Last year James Jones spent $34,000 which was far in excess of what was deductible from his income....

NO ONE HAS PAID A DIME TOWARD THEIR KEEP—not even buying of cigarettes, shows—or an occasional feed at a restaurant in Terre Haute. Everything, even a few pairs of shoes and if clothes are needed are furnished for those who enter....

—Courtesy of University of Illinois at Springfield Archives

[Lowney wrote these notes quickly on the day before she and two other Colonists left for winter quarters. Apparently the magazine did not accept her article. She wrote on the manuscript "not used—rewritten 11-23-'52." Curiously, Lowney does not give details about her method of teaching, including copying. Jones on November 24, 1952, seemingly using Lowney's notes, rewrote the account of the Colony, but that piece also was not published, either. Twenty-two students, some only briefly, were at the Colony in 1952. —EDS.]

DON SACKRIDER

EXTRACTS FROM A [MARCH 15, 1950,] LETTER TO DON SACKRIDER FROM LOWNEY HANDY

Dear Don:

Your letter just came—and maybe you're trying to do too much—absorb all of Washington in a few weeks.

Remember this—take IT EASY—you get a better perspective that way. ALSO EVERYTHING IS AN ILLUSION. Don't let people upset you with their problems. At least don't let ANYTHING OR ANYONE touch half of your mind. You've got to remain critical and things are never all good or bad—never all absolutely true—because no person can see all there is to a problem. The very thing I'm trying hard to teach you now—not Army—not material (You've got so much now you are inarticulate) but to see the rounded viewpoint. Don't go all out for Tom. WHO YET HAS LIVED ENOUGH TO TELL YOU HOW TO THINK OR WHERE TO DIE?

Did I write you that the Lt wrote your mother (it came here to your brother so ask him about the letter he forwarded on to her) telling her you were officer material. Jim thinks you need to become one so you can get a rounded viewpoint and it will give you another field to write about. He's limited to that one....

There is no more than a hair's breadth between the artist and the criminal. When Jim first took the test here—when he first came—he registered criminal. That didn't surprise me at all—for I had already told him that was what he was. The army (especially the enlisted man—or most of them) are of criminal tendencies. Don't let that worry you—the artist graduates out of the criminal class and looks into his heart and writes—or else he watches those around him with a cold clinical eye and writes about himself as he sees them. That is the way Jim writes....

Are you doing your SCIENCE OF BREATH—deep breathing exercises—get a copy if you don't have one and re-read—you'll be surprised at what you overlooked....

—Courtesy of Don Sackrider

[Don was in the Army in 1950. He did not become an officer; instead, he left the Army and returned to the Colony. —EDS.]

To Spite Your Own Face was written while I was in basic training in the Army in 1949. I polished the story while I was with Lowney Handy, Jim Jones, and Will Lindsay in New Mexico on my first furlough.

Of course, Lowney and Jim gave me a lot of feedback while I was there, cutting and trimming. The story was ready to make the rounds by the time my furlough ended. Jim wrote a letter to the agent, Diarmuid Russell, and he agreed to handle the story. I went up to New York on a pass from the Army while I was stationed in Washington, D.C., and had lunch with Russell. The story made the rounds of several magazines but was never published.

For some reason, we, or I, never pushed the story after I got out of the Army. I think it could have become a basis for a novel, now that I look back. There were a lot of fellows in the Army at that time who did not make great scores on the Army Intelligence Tests, and I think the reason was that some of the good scores are related to sophistication. Many of these fellows from the mountains had not seen much of the world outside their own state. This was before television introduced the world to everyone.

When I left the Colony and eventually gave up writing to pursue a career as a pilot, I burned the novel I was working on. For some reason, this story survived the fire.

—Don Sackrider

To Spite Your Own Face

By Don Sackrider

Dick Revere came back to Recruit Barracks from noon chow with another different helmet liner. This was the third one somebody had switched on him. By the time he got out of basic, Revere calculated, he would have been the possessor of eight different dilapidated liners if it kept on at the present rate.

Chicken Haley got up from his bunk behind one of the pillars and headed for Revere's locker. "Let's get out tonight!" Chicken's boyish face was twisted eagerly.

He took Revere by the arm, "Buddy, I can't stand no more of this. A man might as well be in jail." Their third week of intense infantry training, entering in a July heat wave, had not erased the boy's Bluefield mine pallor. Although it had seemed to broaden his shoulders and the sun had added a light to his eyes. A frantic light now.

"Relax!" Revere sat down on his locker. "Relax, Chicken." He adjusted the headband of the liner and tried it. "In another week we'll be eligible for a pass. You heard what the Old Man said."

"What's the matter?" Haley jeered. "You ain't scared?" He sat down on Revere's bunk and looked up at Revere owlishly.

"Get up off my goddamn bunk," Revere said. Haley got up. "After what happened today," Chicken Haley said, "you don't think they'll give you a pass?"

"My nose is clean. I'm not going to get myself on their scab list," Revere said, smoothing the blanket free of wrinkles. "You know, AWOLs never get chances for a pass." He stood back and inspected the freshly tailored bunk.

"What can they do to you?" Chicken insisted. "What did the others get?"

"Not much the first time."

"That's what I say. And I can't wait no week!" Chicken socked his fist into his palm. "I got to have me a woman!"

"You're working damned hard, Chicken," Revere said, "just to keep people from finding out you're fourteen." The idea of going AWOL was not so horrifying to Dick Revere because he told himself that he might go AWOL before his enlistment was up. You heard so much about AWOL it became a part of your thinking. But to do anything with Haley was too much like contributing to the delinquency of a minor. Haley probably wouldn't go unless he went with him. He'd be doing Haley a favor to say no.

"I still don't see how you lied so well," Revere told Chicken. "I bet you still hang up your stocking at Christmas."

"Damn you. I can take anything you can and you know it. But I didn't join no army to lose my self-respect." Chicken glared at Revere hotly.

Chicken had taken a hell of a razzing about his age. But he had stood up to the training like a man with the best of the eighteen-year-old recruits.

From out in the company area someone sounded off yelling, "Mail Call," and Revere moved to the window to check on its authenticity. Somebody was always yelling a dry-run Mail Call. Outside nobody was paying any attention, and the men were returning from chow. The rest of the day was scheduled for Preliminary Rifle Instruction on the dry range with its long hours of practice sighting, crouched in the dust without the excitement of live ammunition. Revere saw Porky Lansing coming up the steps of the barracks.

"Did I have any mail, Porky?" Revere asked him.

"I don't know," the fat boy grinned. "It was a dry run." Then he saw it was Revere. "Hey, man! They done yelled for you and Haley on the box just as I was leaving the chow house."

"The orderly room?" Revere questioned.

"Yes, old buddies," Porky grinned. "You're going to catch it now. You'll learn to talk back to chaplains."

"I hope so," Molotovich said from behind him. Molotovich had been made trainee assistant to the platoon sergeant.

"Go to hell, Bigfeet," Haley said from Revere's locker.

"Don't tell me to go to hell," Molotovich warned tightly.

"That's right," Porky told Haley. "Bigfeet is a corporal now." He nodded toward the black arm band with the stripes on it pinned around Molotovich's sleeve.

"Next time they go making us look bad in front of the chaplain," Molotovich said, "we'll take care of them."

"Go blow it out your stack, Bigfeet," Porky said. "You're as wishy-washy as them runny eggs they give us. In fact, with them feet you'd make a good eggbeater."

"Okay, Lardass," Molotovich said, "get ready to fall out. You're supposed to take orders from me the same as if I was a real corporal." He turned to Tick Hoover who had just come in. "He's in your squad, Hoover. Make him get ready. I want every man out there when the whistle blows."

"Kiss this!" Porky said. "You're no different than the rest of us recruits."

"That's a telling him," Tick Hoover said and stretched out across a couple of lockers and stared at the ceiling.

Porky caressed his front bulge. "My gut is full. I had thirds on that stew today, besides half of Revere's. I don't feel like falling out today."

"You better watch it," Molotovich warned Tick narrowly. "You don't get on the ball, you'll get yourself busted."

"Busted!" Tick snickered. "Who cares. I'm just a TS acting corporal."

"And you two men," Molotovich said to Revere and Haley, "better get your butts over to the orderly room. Molotovich moved off upstairs to check on the rest of the platoon.

"Busted," Tick Hoover said again. "I wish I would get busted, by god. I wish I was a rear-rank eight ball in the awkward squad."

"Forget it. You're okay," Porky said.

"You're about the only one thinks so," Tick said dreamily. "I hope I would get busted."

"One week from tomorrow. Boy!" Porky wheezed one of his typical chuckles. "Passes. Am I going to get soused!"

"What on?" Tick wanted to know. "Pay day ain't till a week from Monday."

"I'm expecting a letter," Porky grinned.

"All that's holding me up is money," Tick said. "If I had money, I'd really get myself busted."

"Why all the sudden interest in getting yourself busted?" Revere asked.

"Because, my scholarly friend," Tick said getting up, "I would rather be liked than be a lieutenant. But you wouldn't know about that, would you?"

"Why wouldn't I?"

"Because you're too scholarly, I reckon," Tick said.

"Come on, Revere," Chicken Haley said nervously. "We better get over to the orderly room."

"All right, you men!" Tick hollered. "Off your seat and on your feet! Get ready to fall out."

"What's coming off?" Haley said as they went out the door.

Revere shook his head. "You know as much as I do."

"We're in for it now."

"My nose is clean," Revere said.

"So's mine," Chicken said doggedly. "Mine's cleaner than yours.

When that chaplain up and asked for special gripes, at least I give him a real one. Everybody hates them raw eggs they give us for breakfast that ain't even half-cooked; they just didn't nobody have as much guts as me, that's all. But who the hell ever heard of anybody griping about a 'balanced diet' like you did? A 'balanced diet,' for Christ's sake."

"So what?" Revere said irritably. "It isn't balanced."

"Tastes all right to me," Chicken said. "Except for them eggs."

"The truth is," Revere said, "we were both damned fools for sounding off at all."

"That's just what I mean," Haley said eagerly. "You and me won't never get no pass now. The only way we'll get a pass is if we take one."

Revere stopped walking and turned on him. "Do you want to go AWOL, Haley?"

"You're goddamn right," Chicken Haley said stoutly. "We'll show them they can't treat a man like this."

"Give me a coin," Revere said.

"Tonight!" Chicken said. "Let's go tonight."

"Relax, why don't you?" Revere said.

"Just for a couple of days," Chicken said. "I don't care what they do. It'd be worth it."

"We couldn't go home," Revere said. "That's the first place they'd look. Besides, we haven't any money."

"I'll pay your way," Chicken said. "I got ten bucks. I know a cabin up in the hills close to home. It ain't more than a hundred miles from here."

"All right," Revere said. "Give me a coin."

"You're chicken," Chicken Haley said. "You're yellow to go."

"No," Revere said. "I'm not yellow. Give me a quarter, I said. If it comes heads, I go; tails, I stay."

Haley looked at him disbelievingly. "You mean you'll let the coin decide for you?"

"Sure," Revere grinned. "I always decide important decisions that way."

"You're screwy," Haley said. "You know what's wrong with you, Revere?" He said mockingly. "You're a goddamn intellectual."

"You think so?" Revere said. "Give me the coin."

"Let me flip it," Haley said nervously.

"Go ahead then. Flip it."

"All right," Haley shrugged. He flipped the quarter into the air and watched it, fascinated, as it fell on the walk. It was heads.

"You're really going then?" Chicken Haley said disbelievingly. "Maybe you better think it over."

"It was heads, wasn't it?" Revere said coolly. "I always stick by my coin." Why not foul up? Who wanted to be classed as an intellectual. It was just because they made him work in the orderly room.

"Do you want to go," Revere said contemptuously, "or don't you?"

"Sure I want to go."

"Okay, come on then. We'd better get over to the orderly room now."

2

The signal to fall out sounded as Revere was knocking on the orderly room door.

"Come in," the clerk said. His name was Ratner but most of the trainees didn't know him by name. He looked up from his typewriter and scratched his ear.

"Haley, you're to report to the mess hall for the rest of the day. Revere, the first sergeant said I could have you to work for me in here."

Haley eyed Revere.

"Okay, Haley," Ratner said. "Move it!"

"Yes, Sir," Haley said nervously.

"These green men." Ratner grinned at Revere as he put him to work. "When'll they ever learn you don't call a non-com 'Sir'?"

Revere didn't say anything. Under the circumstances, since it was Haley's money that they were going on, he felt he ought not to say anything disloyal.

He worked all afternoon on forms for the trainees. It wasn't very hard work. The first sergeant was off having coffee someplace. When the afternoon mail came in, Ratner took some letters into the captain's office, and Revere took a break for a smoke.

Apparently, never a day went by without a letter from some recruit's mother, or mama, or dear maw. It seemed none of the recruits had any fathers; at least they never wrote any letters. Women were the letter writers, Revere decided, recalling the one yesterday that the office had howled over:

I is Sam's only mother and I think I art to have some money as he said I would when I let him go. He has only this one mother. Please see if the Captain don't think I art to have some of his money.

Only one mother ... I art to have some money ... get me some money. It was a surprisingly recurrent theme, Revere grinned, listening to them in the other office.

"This man Haley," Ratner was saying. "The fourteen-year-old minority. You remember we wrote to his mother asking for his birth certificate so we could discharge him. Now she writes back saying isn't there some way to keep him in the Army. His father was killed in the mine and she's got children and not much able to work. She says she can't keep him off the streets at home and he won't work and she needs the money from his allotment."

"Jesus Christ!" The captain's voice boomed through the partition.

Revere decided to excuse the hypocrisy, in this case, in spite of the captain's fatherly lectures on abstaining from the use of profanity. Revere clinched his cigarette and put the butt in his pocket.

"Taking it easy, Revere?" the first sergeant said from the door.

Revere grinned and went back to work.

"We're going to make a soldier out of this guy yet," the first sergeant said to Ratner as the clerk came out of the other office. "He not only takes a break to smoke one of your cigarettes as soon as you're gone, but he clinches the butt and puts it away in his pocket."

"He's a good boy," Ratner smiled sportingly.

The talk in the orderly room was of the passes next weekend. It was the only thing the trainees could think of, and even the permanent party men couldn't stay away from it.

The clerk nodded toward the captain's office. "He wants you to give the company your best five-minute lecture on pass policy some time soon," Ratner told the first sergeant.

WRITINGS FROM THE HANDY COLONY

The first sergeant held up three fingers. "No liquor, no women, so swearing," he said, ticking them off. "Remember that, Revere."

"I won't be needing a pass," Revere said. "I'm going AWOL." He laughed.

"What's the matter," Ratner grinned. "Can't you think of something original?"

Revere laughed down in his belly. He wondered if he could get away with murder.

"I'm homesick," he told Ratner. "Or hard up for a woman. That's always a good excuse for AWOL."

"What's all this?" the first sergeant said from his desk.

"I'm just being talked out of going AWOL," Revere said.

"When Revere goes over the hill you can make out my overseas papers, Ratner," the first sergeant grinned.

"Is that a compliment, Sergeant?" Revere said. "Or a dig?"

"Figuring AWOL percentage on resistance and force, and speaking mathematically, you'd be the last to jump the fence."

"I wonder if first sergeants ever go AWOL?" Revere asked with ravishment.

"Not when they're getting as short as I am," the first sergeant said.

"If Revere was as near to a discharge as you are," Ratner grinned, "he might go over the hill. I might go myself."

"Not Revere," the first sergeant grinned.

"The sergeant classes me with white mice," Revere told Ratner.

Ratner threw up his hands. "It's getting over my head," he said, tearing into his work.

They let Revere off at 4:30. But the first sergeant let him hang around five minutes more so he could miss the 4:35 retreat formation. After he showered, Revere stood on the barracks porch safely within the shade and listened for the troops to return from retreat.

Over and across the yard, he saw Haley come out of the mess hall. Revere started inside the barracks.

"Lucky!" Haley called.

"Who says?" Revere said and sprawled out on the banister and glanced up at the sky.

"You'll get one next week, though, won't you?" Haley hinted, and puffed his cigarette jerkily. The mess sergeant yelled at him, and he squeezed out the butt and returned inside.

Haley bothered Revere. This afternoon Ratner had said he would make sure Revere got a pass if he wanted it. There wouldn't be much to having a pass without money, though. Both he and Haley had been caught in the chaplain's trainee trap, but Haley got a KP out of it and Revere got to work in the orderly room. Haley would picture him typing on a pleasant afternoon helping Ratner where it was cool and there was leftover lemonade from noon chow.

Actually, it had been suffocating in the little box that was the orderly room. Revere was more than glad to get out of it. He had smoked too many of Ratner's free cigarettes, not wanting them. He had been eating too much lately, too; as always, he decided, he made a fool out of himself when something was free.

He watched a whirlpool of dust in the street agitating the dead air. A sudden, powerful gust swooped the particles toward the porch. Revere turned his face. At last it started to rain.

Up and down sheets of rain swept across the roof of the mess hall. The wind changed and the pattern criss-crossed. In the distance, the returning troops would be rushing the cadence now, Revere thought. He stepped inside the barracks to keep from being trampled by the rush of sweat- and rain-soaked men.

"Restricted tonight!" Tick Hoover threw his helmet liner on the floor. "And another clean uniform shot to hell!"

"How restricted?" Revere asked.

"You weren't there, were you?" Tick said. "Just wait till you see how I get myself busted."

"'Cause so many of 'em passed out at retreat." It was George Shoate who answered. "At least, I guess that's the reason. Even Lt. Warner passed out."

"I bet we're going to set the record for all-time AWOLs in the company," Tick said. "Boy, did Sgt. Rooney chew me out this afternoon."

"Tick, my boy," Shoate grinned, "that's what we get for being squad leaders."

"I'm going to quit," Tick said.

"I done ask the sergeant could I quit," Shoate said dolefully. "He said I had to give him ten days notice, and when that ten days was up I could just give him ten more." He slapped Tick on the back. "Yes,

Sir, I tell you, buddy, we're screwed. But at least we don't have no KP like Revere here."

"KP ain't so bad," Revere said.

"Anybody wants my job can have it." Tick raised his voice and reached for the cigarette butt in Shoate's hand. "I'd rather have friends. I'm going to mess up."

"And cut off your own nose," Shoate said. "Come on. We'll buck the chow line. Cheer you up."

"I don't want to eat." Tick kicked the foot locker.

Someone in the far end of the barracks cried attention, but Lt. Day was already past the first few bunks. It was another minute before the men got to their feet.

"At ease," Lt. Day said anyway. "I know someone is always fooling around yelling 'Attention,' but just the same it pays to look around and be on the safe side, men."

Revere supposed that last night's instance had gotten back to the orderly room. The recruits had played a game with the company's mail clerk, calling attention every time he entered the barracks. After it happened half a dozen times, the officer in charge of quarters came through, and when someone yelled attention, Shoate had yelled back, "Don't call attention for that little bastard!" Roaring with laughter, until Tick pulled him up on his feet. "Some joker's going to get us in trouble if they don't watch out," Shoate had said unhappily.

Lt. Day motioned for Revere to come with him.

"I've some work to do on lessons for tomorrow," Lt. Day told Revere. "If you don't mind helping me again. And I understand you are still restricted again tonight, anyway. I'll see that your rifle is cleaned."

Revere hung back. "Sir, I could clean it now in a few minutes if it's all right."

Lt. Day laughed. "You're too valuable a man. Come in the back way, and I'll have them let you eat first."

As Revere left the mess hall, Haley called him over to the sink.

"Tonight!" Haley whispered viciously. "Don't chicken out."

"I'll stick," Revere said. "I've got to work for the lieutenant right now. I'll see you in the barracks tonight."

"Don't forget, goddamn you!" Chicken said, "Lieutenant or no goddamn lieutenant!"

3

Revere seated himself at one of the officer's desks next to Lt. Day. It was a while before Lt. Day looked up from his papers.

"You know, what you did in that chaplain's class this morning was pretty silly," the lieutenant said.

Revere grinned at him. "But I did know what I was talking about, Sir."

"Perhaps," Lt. Day put his pen down, shoved the papers back. "But the chaplain was just stuck with time and was trying to fill in the class."

These last few times Revere had worked with Lt. Day they had talked together on an equal plane more or less, discussing the summer theater in the city, to which the lieutenant and his wife had season tickets and went every Friday night.

"You can always come to me and talk over anything," Lt. Day said.

"Thank you, Sir. Maybe you can do something about the eggs then, Sir."

"We're looking into that," Lt. Day promised. "How do you find you get along with so little sleep?"

"That was one thing I got plenty of," Revere told him. "I think I'm less keen mentally when I lose sleep."

"Perhaps," Lt. Day disagreed. "However, I find that an extra meal will provide the needed energy." This wasn't a new topic. Lt. Day related again the tale of working through college and studying at night.

"I did that for four years and made it just as well. After work I'd take a midnight supper and get my lessons for the morning. And not to brag, but I was an honor student. Look how Ford and Edison and some of those boys got along on so little sleep."

"They had notoriously slow heart beats," Revere cited. He decided that the lieutenant also had him pegged for an intellectual. He switched his approach.

"I ain't that well off, Sir," Revere said with a straight face. "They comes a time when I can't do nothing without no sleep."

Lt. Day was silent after that. Finally he went off to the Club and left Revere working at the typewriter. He was still working when the first sergeant looked in to pick up his pipe.

"I guess I was right about the white mouse," the first said.

"I love the work here," Revere said, "and I just can't tear myself away." It was sarcastic, he knew; trainees didn't talk to first sergeants that way. But he also knew the first expected him to talk that way. And that white mouse business was getting under his skin.

It was 7:30 when Revere got back to the barracks. His rifle had not been cleaned. To hell with it, he thought, I won't be needing a rifle anyway. He went to look up Haley.

Chicken Haley was not at this bunk.

"Where's Chicken?" Revere asked Shoate, who was sitting by himself on his own bunk, contentedly rolling his dice.

"Went over to D Company to see a old buddy from his home-town." Shoate grinned at him. "Guess he's got the blues. What are you doin' tonight?"

"I'm a white mouse," Revere told him. "Caught in this cage of Restriction, just like the rest of you white mouses. Only, I think this white mouse is going to bust out of his trap."

"Let's you and me go get drunk then," Shoate grinned.

"Yeah?" Revere said. "On what?"

"I been lucky," Shoate said. He flipped the dice between his fingers. "Now tell me what's on the other side." With another flipping of the fingers the numbers on the dice changed again. "Now tell me."

"Who'd you take?" Revere asked.

"Chicken Haley. He was loaded. Ten bucks."

"Goddamn you, Shoate! You ought to be ashamed. Chicken isn't old enough to know boxcars from fever." Revere couldn't help feeling angry. There goes your orgy, pal, he told himself, because Chicken's done shot his wad.

"He's old enough to know better than to gamble with me, though."

Shoate's eyes sparkled. He flipped the dice. "Well, are you going or ain't you?"

"When are we going?" Revere said. He was beginning to believe he was a white mouse. Resistance and Force. Turn on the current and see how many will cross it.

"I said when are we going?"

"Right now," Shoate said. "So's we'll have plenty of time to get good and soused. You and me and Tick."

"Tick!" Revere said.

Tick came over and flopped on Shoate's pillow. "Did I hear my name given the blame? Did you holler, Scholar?"

"He might as well be an eight ball with the rest of us," Shoate said, grinning.

"He already is," Revere said.

"Don't tell them to fall in," Tick mimicked Sgt. Rooney, "just rack them up. They're all eight balls."

The taproom was already filled when they got there. Most of the soldiers were the new recruits. They were always there when they had money and sang loudly over the piles of empty beer glasses. Two or three glasses and most of them were soused.   Revere noticed that a great many didn't look any older than Haley, and he wondered what their mothers who had signed their minority papers would say if they could see their sons now.

Shoate was only seventeen, but he was big and hardy and looked the oldest of them all. He handed Tick some nickels to play the juke box.

"'Tennessee Saturday Night,'" Shoate said.

"Let me play something so I can dream," Tick told him.

It was so noisy they had to take their beer and stand around the juke.

"Memories," Tick said.

"What I need is a woman," Shoate said.

"I've got a couple lined up at home," Tick said, "if I can only get the hell to them."

They went back to the table and started drinking toasts to each other's girl and downed whole glasses of beer at a time because they had to work fast since the Taproom stopped serving at 8:45 and closed at nine o'clock.

"I'm going to get busted tonight," Tick promised. "I want the men to like me. I'd rather be nothing."

"I'd rather be nothing, too," Shoate decided, and they all downed a glass of beer to being nothing.

Revere was tired and the beer tasted flat, but he knew it would spoil everything if he left now. He hadn't been on a chug-a-lug party like this since high school.

"I joined the Army to be a regular fellow like everyone else," Tick explained to them. "And that's what I'm going to do."

Back home his dad had money and a Buick. "I want to be regular." Tick told them.

"Sure," Revere said. "I don't blame you."

"I want you and Shoate to come home with me," Tick said. "You can drive the Buick if you want and we'll have a time."

"And you can buy the beer," Shoate said.

"You don't know what it means for you to buy for me," Tick told him. "At home I was always the one who bought. They liked me because I bought."

"Sure, old buddy," Shoate said. "I understand."

"I wouldn't tell this to anyone but you guys," Tick said.

"We understand," Shoate said.

Revere was silent and drank two more beers.

"I know dozens of women," Tick told them. "Literally dozens. When we get home I'll fix you both up."

"I'll bet you got 'em all knocked up," Shoate said. "Don't you, Revere?"

Tick grinned modestly. "Well, I might have missed a couple."

Two colored soldiers from the quartermaster asked if they could use the extra chair.

"Sure." Shoate said, and almost lifted the chair into the fellow's arms. "What kind of beer you drink?"

Shoate went after refills and put a couple of beers on the table belonging to the colored fellows.

"I'm even feelin' friendly toward the jigs tonight," Shoate said. "What you say we all get drunk tonight?"

4

When they got out of the taxi, Revere started singing.

"Three white mice. See how they drunk. Cut off their nose. Cut off their nose. Cut off their nose."

They staggered in a body toward the barracks.

"They're drunk," two or three of the fellows yelled. "We'll get to toss them in the shower."

Revere went first. They gave him a gleeful test. Porky held up Revere's thumb.

"What's the number of this finger?"

"First."

"He's drunk," Porky decided. "Throw him in. It's your thumb, dummy."

"You never took piano lessons," Revere laughed, struggling. "In music it's your first."

They shook their heads, grinning.

Revere was cold sober when he came out of the shower. He did not think he had ever been so happy in his life. He noticed that Shoate was standing beside him drying off.

"Where's Tick?" Revere asked.

"I think they're having trouble with him in the shower," Shoate told him, grinning.

"We'd better see," Revere said.

They went to get dry shorts out of their lockers. When Revere looked around, Shoate was passed out on his bunk.

In the latrine some of the fellows were trying to get Tick on a toilet. Each time he fell on the floor.

Revere went over to take charge. There was a silly grin on Tick's face, and with his eyes closed he was swatting at the fellows like flies and they stood laughing.

Revere lifted Tick's face trying to talk to him, but he could not get past the grin.

"Hey!" Porky yelled. "Sgt. Rooney's on his way over. Better get him sobered up quick."

Revere slapped Tick across the face. The cat-eating-cream grin was still peering at him ludicrously when Sgt. Rooney stepped into the latrine.

Rooney put his hand on his hip and stared at them.

"Better get him sobered up quick. I don't care how you do it, but keep it quiet and do it quick."

Under Sgt. Rooney's stare they got Tick into the shower room. Revere hadn't the strength to hold him, and Tick lay on the floor sputtering under the cold water. When they turned off the tap, he sat up and started pounding the water out of his ears.

"Good deal!" He laughed hilariously. "I'll be busted tomorrow for sure. Good deal!"

"Revere," Sgt. Rooney said solemnly, "first of all I want to thank you for taking care of my drunks. When and if Hoover sobers up, you can tell him for me that he will be busted tomorrow for sure."

"I was with them," Revere said.

"And for that I give you my heartiest thanks," Sgt. Rooney told him.

"But you don't understand," Revere said. "I was drunk, too. They threw me in the shower first. I was drunk, too."

"Don't try to cover up for them," Sgt. Rooney advised him. "They ain't worth it." He looked around. "All right, you men. Let's hit the sack."

As he left, Sgt. Rooney told Revere he was to work in the orderly room tomorrow all day, but to take time off to clean his rifle.

Tick was sober now, but he was still laughing happily. "I'll be busted tomorrow for sure. You heard him. Happy day!"

"No, you won't," Revere said. "If you'd been sober you'd have seen that Rooney was more than half tight himself."

"Not that tight," Porky said. "Well, Tick, my boy," he wheezed a chuckle, "you did it. My, I bet old Revere will be a rough one when they make him acting corporal."

"I won't take it," Revere said.

"Why, you know the lieutenant's fair-haired boy wouldn't get drunk and mess up," Porky grinned. "Nobody would ever believe that."

"I said I won't take it," Revere said. "I won't take it, by god. I was drunk, too. I told him that. You know I was drunk, too."

When I was in high school, it was still the Big Band era. A group of students had their own dance band. I did not play in that band, but I hung out with some of them. We hitchhiked to Chicago and St. Louis to hear the Big Bands like Stan Kenton, the Dorseys and Harry James.

We bought Down Beat *magazine to read where the bands were playing around the country and to read news about their latest recordings. Our hair was a little long for those times, musician-style, and we read books about jazz like,* Really the Blues. *So far as I know, we did not have marijuana in school then. We probably would have tried marijuana had it been available.*

I wrote this story a year or two out of high school when I thought I was looking back with some objectivity at the band members. Now, with more than fifty years of objectivity, I see it was drawn from me as much as anyone in that band of Hep musicians.

—Don Sackrider

ODE TO THE WEST

By Don Sackrider

As soon as the last set was over, the band members collected their money and piled outside the stage door, jamming instruments and stands and themselves into cars. With their cut from the job, the blond young man and the young, dark-haired girl slipped away from the rest of them, around to the front of the ballroom and caught a taxi.

"Where were they going?"

"To Kelly's for drinks," he said. "I don't think they'll even miss us."

"It's wonderful," she said meeting his eyes in the hinged hollowness of the cab. "To be gone from them."

"Ummhmm," he said and slid his arm across the coolness of the leather, around behind her. "We are on our way, sweet. To that private desert island."

"Lush and tropical," she said. "With coconut palms and cockatoos and all the rest but with no people."

Her lips and his glasses got in the way and he slipped them off and into his pocket.

"That's better," she said.

"The glasses," he whispered.

"The tropical island, you dope," her words melted on his mouth.

He kissed her again, paying no attention to the streets through which they moved.

The taxi pulled up in front of a hotel, one of those along the lakefront that made the city popular, especially in summer. The squat driver put their bags on the curb. Looking at the meter, he took a puff on his cigarette and held out a hand.

In the cool early December night, Archie Sappenfield felt wonderful. The skyline was filled with flashing neon signs that guaranteed a bright and tasty life. He looked at Ellen, standing beside him quietly like a warm energy-giving sun.

"A good hotel is important," he said. The windowed cliffs rose protectively above him. "A good hotel makes you feel rich—chocolate rich, not money rich. A cheap one makes you feel cheap. This is a good one. I've stayed here before."

They stood under the canopy, admiring each other comfortably, the wind blowing in their hair. In its rain-splattered voice the night told him the swift moving pace of the earth was a thing to love, a thing free and forever unstained by even history. Ervie, a joe he knew, living in a fog of *Time* magazine history couldn't see the real life.

"It looks like the place where we stayed in Cleveland," Ellen said. She pointed at the "Grill" sign on the hotel corner. "Even that's the same."

"You wait in there while I get the room, honey." Arch reached into his pocket for a comb to slick back his hair, cut long musician-style and looking like a wet yellow chamois, and put his glasses back on. He walked through the revolving doors and was cramped by the huge sax case and the overnight bag, bumping them he lifted them high and tucked them close.

It was after one and the lobby was no more than dimly lit. An energetic vacuum was guiding a foot-sore porter through vagrant patches of light on the wilted rugs. Another clean-up man leaned forward in mid-stride to clear a thumb-worn magazine from the floor.

"I want a room," Arch said at the desk.

"Yes, Sir. Single or double?"

Arch looked at the clerk, then at the elevators that were hidden around the corner toward the grill.

"A single."

"Yes, Sir," the clerk said. "Sign right here," and slapped his open palm down on the service bell.

Two hands glued themselves to the bags and the bell hop said, "This way please."

"Second. Hold it," Arch said, stopping in front of the single elevator that was open and lighted. "Be right back."

Ellen was standing just inside the grill and she smiled, her clear eyes brightening when she saw him. On a job, he thought, she always looks so stern and tense, but now—and it always surprised him—her face is soft and her lips are full.

"Hello, darling," she said. She squeezed her arm in his as they walked back and into the elevator. The hop closed the iron work filigree giving Arch a faint one-sided smile. Arch looked away finding his comb and ran it through his hair using both hands.

"Looks like you've been blowing the horn tonight," the hop said, eyeing the sax case.

"Yeah. We played a job out at the Troc tonight," Arch informed him. "House band's night off. There's no school tomorrow so we decided to stay over."

"You from State U?"

"Yeah," Arch said, then wishing he hadn't mentioned school. He put a finger up to his mustache wondering if it needed darkening again.

"Thought I remembered you," the hop said guardedly. "I caught your outfit a couple weeks ago. You going to school down there on the GI?"

"Not me," Arch said. "I'm not that lucky. The war come along too late to deal me in."

"Me, too," the hop said. He relaxed picking up the lament. "Them GIs got it soft. I'd like to be going to school drawing down money from the government. Big schools so crowded with GIs us civilians can't even get in now. I decided to go to business school here in town."

"Yeah. You have to know the president or somebody on the board of directors to get in the big schools anymore," Arch said. "That's how I got in."

"And I don't know somebody who knows somebody," the hop said with a tinge of sarcasm.

"I was accepted at the last minute," Ellen laughed politely. "I guess I was lucky, too."

"You got your looks," Arch grinned.

"You and me got drummed out of the good deals," he looked at the hop. "I guess we're just another lost generation, it looks like." He could feel the hop really taking him in then, and he automatically looked in the elevator mirror. There was a satisfaction in the musician haircut and thick musician's glasses framed by the powder blue cardigan coat with no lapels and wide shoulders and the long loose drape. He grinned and flashed the gold-capped teeth. He looked like what he was. "What did you think of the band?"

"Fine. That the new *Down Beat* you got there?"

"Yeah. Just out." Arch slapped the bulky patch pocket. "What did you think of those riffs we pulled off between numbers?"

"Pretty damn good. Kenton still ahead in the *Beat* band poll?"

"Way ahead," Arch said. "Nearly three to one lead over Ellington, who's running second. You should've heard Kenton's concert he gave down at school. Man, he makes our arrangements sound like a barn-yard dress rehearsal."

"I caught him down there. You bet. I'd walk a thousand miles to hear him. What a sock outfit."

"You got to hand it to that crew," Arch said. "As Kenton says, bands with guts will play what they like."

"Yeah" the hop said, "even if the grass is greener on the commercial side of the hill."

"That's the trouble with us," Arch said. "We pull down good enough dough, but we got to curtsey and cater to these peasants who go for the moody and mellow mush, like Vomit Monroe. I wish our band could dictate terms the way Kenton does."

"You heard this latest disc of Kenton's?" the hop pounced him. "There's something to live for. It blots me right out of this universe."

"Terrific," Arch said, "both sides. I had the first pressing on campus."

They walked out of the elevator and down the long corridor of blue and wine pastel. The hop turned the key in the lock, clattering the tag, and opened the light varnished door.

The snap of the light showed them a room in the same soft blue and wine pastels smelling clean of heavy wax.

"It isn't as nice as I figured," Arch said in an undertone when the hop went to check the bath.

Ellen sat down on one of the beds. "I think it's lovely."

The hop walked to the windows to adjust the blinds. "I bet you play piano," he said, looking over his shoulder at Ellen.

"Yes," she said, not surprised and leaning back on awkwardly but luxuriously outstretched arms. "Not so progressively as Kenton though," she laughed. "You really seem to like him."

"You bet. I worship that man. He's a real powerhouse."

"We're no pagans either." Arch put his arm around Ellen. "We worship him even more so, don't we, honey?"

"It was Arch who taught me appreciation of modern music," she said. "I'm afraid I was a bit outdated."

"There's no hope for the old music," Arch said with sagacity. "More and more people are getting tired of it." He looked at the hop levelly. "The world needs strong music, so let 'em have it. A couple of years will tell the tale."

"Where did you latch onto that tie?" the hop said, shuttling the key from one had to the other. "I've never seen anything like it before."

"A friend of mine who designs costumes painted it for me," Arch said. "You see the white dove represents the artist freeing himself from convention and society." Walking over to the hop and digging for change at the same time, he pointed at a huge cross bone skull. "That's convention and society. The orange eye represents freedom of expression." He watched the hop's reaction.

The hop studied it dubiously. "I guess that sums up what a guy like Kenton means to me."

"Exactly," Arch said, drawing his hand out of his pocket with a half dollar in it. The hop handed him the key and backed smoothly out of the room.

"Intelligent guy. He knows his music," Arch said giving the night lock a quick click. "I liked him."

"He seemed very much impressed with you," Ellen said. "Talking the same music and you playing in a band and all."

"There's a genuine 'alligator' for you," he told her. "Appreciates fine music even though he's not a musician. He's more enthusiastic than some of the fellows I know who call themselves cats. Like Ervie Reinoehl out in Fleming City. Always listening to baseball games when he isn't at this piano."

"Like me before you taught me," Ellen said.

"But you had the ability, honey. You're on the right path now. You were bound to come to it sooner or later." He flipped off the fright light that burned from the ceiling and turned on the soft desk light that glowed an orange dusk from its paper shade. Pulling her to her feet, he found her lips to be taken. Their voices, sinking, became velvet whispers blending with the muted rain exhausting itself on the window glass. Rising and dying again it whispered the knowledge it had gained on all the seas and rivers in the world. It whispered beauty that led the soul into a heaven of pure yet passionate ecstasy.

He lay relaxed in her warmth and felt nothing was more wonderful than this, not even when he was on the stand in his private ecstasy. Love is what makes a man, he thought, from love he draws the notes to sing his songs. That was what Ervie didn't know.

"I think I could go like this forever," he said.

"Yes," Ellen said sleepily. "Me, too. As long as I know you really need me. You do need me. Don't you, Arch?"

"Sure," Arch said. "Say. Want me to send down for some Cokes? I got a pint along." He got up and pulled it from his coat on the chair.

"Umnn," Ellen yawned. "We'd never get rid of that hop if he came back up and you both get started on Kenton again."

"I thought he was an all right guy," Arch said. "I thought you liked him."

"Did, darling," she wrinkled her nose at him. "But in small doses."

"Now why do you say that?"

"Well," Ellen said, "because, nitwit—I want to be with you myself."

"You're my chicken," Arch said. "But he's strong for Kenton."

"And anyway," Ellen said, "I think he's pretty small potatoes."

"Well, he really dug that tie of mine," Arch insisted.

"Yes," she said reluctantly.

"And he caught those symbols right away, too. Not many people do that, you know."

38

"That's the tie Bert Stone painted for you isn't it?"

"Yeah."

"He ought to be doing them professionally. Come here and sit beside me," she said smoothing the covers. "What's happened to Bert lately? Why hasn't he been around?"

"Probably loaned out all his money at the Playhouse and can't get down. The jerk."

"Not again."

"I sure pity him." Arch grinned and flicked her hair. "Because he hasn't got an Ellenbaby like me, that's why. Listen, let's drop this Bert riff, okay? I haven't seen him since last Thanksgiving anyway. You know, at Ervie's. When he went out to Fleming City. And if I don't see him till next Thanksgiving, that's okay by me, too."

"But I thought you went out to Ervie's by yourself," she said. She stared at him with wonder. "Didn't you tell me Bert missed you?"

"He did miss me," Arch declared emphatically. "I rode out with Dad. We waited and waited. Bert didn't call or anything and Dad couldn't wait forever." He pinched his chin. "But Bert had Ervie's address. I'd given him that. Bert hitched out. He was crazy thumbing it in that weather. Looked second cousin to a St. Bernard."

Ellen pulled the covers up and snuggles closer. "Oh, your dad went, too."

"Company convention. Important business contacts." Arch narrowed his eyebrows pushing unripe lines across his forehead. "Bert knew all that. I told him. And when he was late, of course, Dad couldn't wait. And Bert came out alone."

"Well, anyway," Ellen said, "he got there. That was what counted for him to meet Ervie. I am sure he made a good impression."

"You know how Ervie is over new people," he said. "Got to find what makes 'em tick. Like a preacher delving through your sins."

"I only met Ervie that one time," she lowered her long lashes. "With you, honey. He's a character."

"Well, Bert sure made it rough on me. His being there at that time. Ervie was working hard at the piano. He's having a recital up at school," he told her. "Bert kept screwing Ervie up. But Ervie didn't dig that." He licked his lips. "When I mentioned it he just dummied up. He was blowing his lid over Bert's being new. And you know how Bert carries his stuff with him like a one-man show."

He got up and walked around, working his fingers lightly in a fist. "Truly Ervie needed every minute. Bert didn't seem to realize he needed to be alone. It got me frantic."

"You're a musician, darling," Ellen said. "Don't let your voice get so tight." She laughed lightly. "Bert promised to design me a dinner dress. How would you like me in something really shocking, honey? Backless and with a midriff."

"Sure, I'd like you in anything," he said. "But I wouldn't count on Bert. He's always snowed under with work at the Playhouse."

Arch bit at a nail. "Bert's too shrewd and business-like to really make an artist," he said. "You know how Bert talks his designs at all times without caring if you're interested. But I can make an artist out of Ervie."

"Of course you can," Ellen said, lifting the blind to a narrow slip and peering out the window.

In the dark, dripping street below, she could see a policeman standing under a shop awning. He had that appearance of big-city indifference to the snobbish night cat, the four-legged kind, that flitted by him. She snuggled her feet further under the cover.

Arch juggled out a cigarette. "Only thing about Bert," he told her, squinting his eyes to keep the smoke from smarting them, "is he's determined to get ahead. No matter how he gripes, you know someday he'll get all the things he wants. He'll fight the world to the last ditch."

The thought of Bert's determination cut sharply across his mind. It was that same stubborn doggedness that made Bert go out to Fleming City. "But if push comes to shove," he said, "he'd cut anyone's throat. That's why he'll never make an artist. The line between criminal and artist is an infinitesimal line."

"Get me a glass of water will you honey?" Ellen asked.

Arch went into the bath and ran the water cold in the glass. No doubt about it, he thought. Bert sure had Ervie all screwed up out there. Ervie knew practice came before anything else if you wanted to be tops. Ervie was still plenty naive. Bert was new and Ervie had fallen for his smooth, high-jive talk. And then he even had the Boyd's put Bert on a company plane. Fixed it so Bert had flown back.

He handed the glass to Ellen. Then drank heavily from the pint and swallowed the rest of the water as chaser.

"I guess I was really Ervie's first friend," he said, staring into the empty glass. "Back in high school I was the first person to see what he had. I pulled him out of a rut and set him going."

"Personally, I think you are too good to others and neglect your own abilities." She turned her head slowly and looked at him.

"I've been worried about Ervie ever since Thanksgiving. I feel responsible for him, and I'm afraid he's slipping back."

"You're going to really make it yourself someday," she said in a quiet, gold-glinted voice.

"Me? Oh, sure. But you can't pull a fade-out on somebody when just a little attention will keep them going," he said clicking his thumb across the teeth of his pocket comb. "Now you've mentioned him, I'm going to write Ervie right now. Give him a sincere big brother talk."

She watched him obliquely and then looked back at the ceiling.

"Won't take but a few minutes. You won't mind, will you?"

"Go ahead," she said dryly, "if you feel you have to."

Arch ran the comb through the long hair once and sat down at the desk. There was paper with the hotel heading on it in the drawer. The whiskey hadn't worn off yet, and he felt he was going good. Remembering suddenly how he had left the Benzedrine tablets in the other coat, he was surprised. Right now he felt as if he were powered with diesel engines.

Tonight would be the first dance job for a long time he hadn't shaken hands with 'Benny,' but he shouldn't have worried about it. At rehearsal he had slurred the notes quick and easy almost like he did on a benny kick. Everything was just more mellow on benny. I'm glad though now, he thought, plenty glad now; benny and women don't mix much. If I'd had some, I'd be about as much good as a melted candle now.

"You really should have been at last week's job," he wrote. "Kicks galore. I was on lead alto with the campus cats, and the kicks came on like Franklin D and went off like We the People. I had soaked two tablets in a mixture of Four Roses, nutmeg (man that stuff will get you high), some sherry, some more Four Roses, and a touch of baking soda. I don't know why the soda unless I was afraid of indigestion."

Arch tilted back his chair and looked at Ellen. It was nice, he thought, looking at her limp and relaxed body and having her here while he worked.

I downed the wet goods at eight, and by nine when the dance started I had sweat through my powder blue cardigan (man it drapes like mad) and it turned to purple. It was all right the next day though, thank God. By ten my head felt like Grand Central Station during the switch to daylight saving. I was frying hot and burning cold. Flying and crawling. I was ad-libbing to myself like I was Stravinsky playing a Lombardo request broadcast. When the dance ended I was flying but going nowhere, and after we hit some bars and jammed all night I fell in bed exhausted at daylight.

This will knock him out, he thought, picturing the envy on Ervie's face, and then, laughing, he wrote as an afterthought.

When you are ready to die young but happy, try the above recipe.

"Honey, are you awake?" he whispered huskily.

"About half," she answered in shadow voice.

"Read this and see what you think," he said, handing Ellen the page.

As he wrote, he could feel the subconscious part of his mind following her progression as she read. He was writing tonight because he felt strongly it was his duty to straighten Ervie out. He and Ervie were buddies and always would be—he hoped. He didn't think he needed to warn Ervie again. He was slipping in a rut. How very proud he'd be when he saw Ervie going after what he wanted with everything he had in him. He had said enough to Ervie Thanksgiving even having his own troubles then.

Ervie might meet him some weekend soon. Maybe catch a good band, Kenton, and find some women. He thought Ervie needed to live a little. It would get him out of his rut and maybe teach him just what the score was. He could tell him a lot of things about Bert, too.

"I thought you hadn't seen Bert lately," she said, her silky voice puzzling.

He laid down the pen and looked at the page she held. "Oh, that was just a selling point to put some things over to Ervie," he explained helpfully. "You know. Ervie was a little sold on Bert."

Arch felt his mind pick up the flow of her reading. The pages under Ellen's eyes, like a phonograph dropping down its records one by one, told Ervie what was good in new music. He had insisted Ervie was to get the new Kenton discs. Plenty he could dig from Kenton's style on the side, "Theme to the West." The other side was a vocal, "Curiosity."

He heard Ellen humming. The words repeated themselves silently. "He said to me ... did you know that ... Curiosity killed the cat."

Ellen was sitting now, bracing her upper body on bent arm and her head in her hand, reading the part with her in it. Arch grinned to himself.

He remembered he had never said these things, not really, to her before. But they were in the letter now. She would read it there. She was a wonderful person and he was very much in love with her. She was unfolding rapidly through her hands at the piano. He was sure that they would inspire each other to play better and better music. They had the same list of faults and got along beautifully, and he was sure he would go further as an artist with her than he would without her. But Ervie ought to be careful. The wrong dame could wreck him. That ought to be enough for this time, he thought, and wound it up with the new Kenton discs again.

Looking over at Ellen, he saw her staring into space and not reading now. She's thinking of what I wrote about her, he thought. He had written it there so she would see.

She looked up as if to say she had finished what he had given her to read.

Looking at the stained ink on his fingers, he smiled faintly and walked into the bath. When he came back, Ellen was up and dressing. "Don't say anything," she said as he stood shirtless in his bleached white skim. "I'm leaving. You only imagined I was here, anyway," she said coldly and snapped shut the overnight bag.

"What do you mean?" He tried to chuckle, waiting for her to turn around and look at him.

"What do I mean?" she whirled back. Her eyes were immovable and dead serious. "I mean you're just like all the other Billy Boys. Running with your tale of troubles to Mother. And if Charming Mother isn't listening, try any old friend." She turned to the mirror and brushed her hair.

His mouth opened tautly. "What do you mean? I always hated my mother's guts."

"Me." Ellen slipped the miniature brush in her purse. "You're trying to hide behind my apron. Or any apron. Aprons are out of date, Billy Boy. At least for me they are."

"What about our music together?" he demanded, his arms trying to grasp her. "Doesn't that mean anything?"

She smoothly avoided him. "Music means everything to me. But not just one kind of music. All I ever hear from you is Kenton. Kenton, Kenton, Kenton. You have failed at everything else so you have built a dream world around Kenton." Her face became a little more tense, but her eyes he saw had that cold calm.

"You never talked this way before," he said stoutly. "Music's my life and Kenton's my music."

"You've run to him as if he were a god instead of a fine musician," she said. "If you aren't careful, you'll make a bobby- sox idol out of him. He'd better watch out. The savages destroy their idols when their gods displease them. Some of you cats are liable to grow claws." She gave a quick glance around the room.

Silence fell on both of them. He felt it all hanging between them like a wall. It was her voice that broke through. "I don't know," she said, and rubbed her hand over her cheek. "But if there is a God to replace the Christianity our generation has lost, it won't be Kenton."

"I thought you loved me, Ellen," he reproached her.

"I guess that is something we both imagined," she said. I guess a woman lives for someone she loves and who needs her. If she doesn't feel really wanted, not needed, the flame inside goes out."

"I do need you," Arch said. "You're wrong."

He watched her fold her arms tightly across her breasts. He thought her eyes looked damp, that she swallowed hard.

"A woman wants to stir approbation and affection," she said. "Have someone really appreciate her." She slipped into her coat and tucked her purse under her arm. "Otherwise she'd rather have your disapproval, dislike even. And concentrate her emotions on someone else."

He ran his fingers disgustedly through his hair. "You've got me so mixed up I don't know what you're trying to say."

"It's very selfish, probably," she said. "In a way it is as selfish as a man always thinking about himself. But that is the way it is, and there isn't anything to do about it."

He made half a gesture toward her.

"No. It's no good, Arch. I'm leaving now. You go ahead and write another of your protégés a letter." Picking up her bag and opening the door all in one movement she was gone.

Arch stared at the door. So this, he thought, this, this is what it's like to have your lover throw you down.

All his pores felt shut and sealed, constipating his nerve ends with body poisons. His fingernails tingles like they'd pop out of the quick. His teeth felt as if he'd just drunk a glass of pure lemon juice. He lay down on the bed choked with exhaustion. But the unanswered reason as to why she left would not let him alone, would not let him sleep.

He didn't want them there but millions of dartings played in and out of his head as gnats after an apple. Then swarming here and there lighting little fires of torment. God! He was really feeling low.

Why did she leave? It came back again and again in a million harsh whispers. He wondered what the hop would think about her walking out like this. Everything was teasing and buzzing and darting in and out and returning always the minute he relaxed. He wanted to reach out and grab all the buzzings and cork them up so he could relax.

Find the truth! He got up grabbing the pint bottle and pushed into the bath. He finished the whiskey and felt the darting buzzings in his stomach. He doubted if he had the strength to find anything. He would go insane trying to find it. Insanity? Horrible word. Insanity was too much imagination. Imagination was good...good if used in moderation, like everything else. Otherwise it might bring hate, fear, love...insanity within seconds.

He threw the bottle on the tile floor. The broken neck bounced back up and cut his leg. It started bleeding. He stooped down and picked up a long sharp sliver of broken glass. He'd read a mystery one. How a man had been murdered with a long thin sliver like this one.

Perhaps it would be better to end it, yes, really end it right here and now. Better to end it and be free. Write a note to her. And Ervie's letter would be found. His last help to Ervie. Ervie would carry on his ideas of music to the world. His own death would force Ervie to grow up.

The darting buzzings were in the leg now, and he felt the burn of the blood trickling down. When resistance ceased the daring buzzings would return, he knew, like gnats after the apple. Then they would eat away until they destroyed the very core of the soul on which they preyed.

Arch looked at the glass in his hand, the lovely beautiful lethal little piece of glass. But he had to stay and fight for his music. She had said he had music to give. He must go on living even in stark tragedy to give music to the world, mustn't he? He put the piece of glass down.

The fellows would still be at Kelly's in a late jam session. He dressed quickly and felt the numbness begin leaving. He had to get out of here. He had to get away. Immerse himself in light, and noise, in a throng of people. Nothing could ever be decided.

What if the boys would see his leg? He could tell them some black had pulled a knife on him. Tell them he was in a honky-tonk out by the Troc and there was a big fight.

As he began to consider what he would tell them, the reflecting vision became a reality. He shuddered to think how close he had escaped death.

Extracts from a February 1950 letter to Don Sackrider from Lowney Handy

Friday
February 1950

Dear Don:

Well here it is. In full. It was quite a blow-but I think I've learned something that we can all use—or those who haven't got going good— and that is throw away your notes. Write out of your subconscious. I'm going to ditch this book completely. Maybe I'll find parts of it creeping into other things I write. But the whole secret is to learn to let it flow out of you. I've not got that yet. The contrived plot stops the characters from—acting normally.

[Lowney then quoted the February 7, 1950, letter of Burroughs Mitchell, editor at Scribner's, to Lowney, rejecting her mystery novel,

But Answer Came There None. *Mitchell found the design of the novel "helter-skelter." Also, he wrote, she did not develop the suspense of the story. A pertinent paragraph from Mitchell's letter is quoted on page 80.—Eps.]*

Saturday. Today I feel better. I know that I haven't put in the necessary work. Also I know that no good work is done when you have a divided mind. Also if you are struggling to build someone up you have to believe they are good. I can't be great when I think someone else is better—it's like that. I'm a little sad—or was—although I know my time will come. Jim [Jones] is anxious to help me. And someday I'll have a book—so will you....

...Try getting little short skits down in your notebook—no matter if they are only a line of two or a paragraph or a page or an incident. I had Jim do this for years before you came along. He's got marvelous notes tucked away. It's what keeps my own writing from coming alive. My characters don't have enough individuality—flair—emotion—conflicts—doing things odd and touching and conflicting—making them human—so take a lesson from me.

Lowney

—*Courtesy of Don Sackrider*

Extracts from an April 10, 1949, letter to Harry Handy from Lowney Handy

Memphis

Dear Harry:

Yesterday I wrote you about the cabin. It was Jim's suggestion and insistence that we place the cabin on the farm...and I wrote at that moment by his strong attitude—as I let myself too often be dominated.

Thinking about it carefully and sleeping over it, I want it at Marshall...I love those woods at the farm and I love not being so easily reached, but that has drawbacks, too. No electricity. And you can-decide it, but I think I'd prefer it back on the Marshall lot. Back in a hollow and out of sight if possible. We can move shrubs in if necessary. But I'll be close to your mother—after all, she did promise to look after me if I was sick—and offered me cash—so if you'll take her into the discussion (I'd like that) and plan a home that is ALL MINE—I'd like that. Not a cabin for others. Jim has his trailer and I'm welcome. And you have the house in Robinson and I'm welcome—but let this be my home—and you will both be welcome.

—Courtesy of University of Illinois at Springfield Archives

[Harry purchased a jeep and trailer for Jones, and in the spring of 1949 Jones and Lowney were in a trailer park in Memphis when the letter was written. Lowney did get her cabin in Marshall, but she was not to be alone there, for it was later decided that the Colony was to be located on the same cow pasture. —EDS.]

EXTRACTS FROM A CIRCA FEBRUARY 1950 LETTER TO DON SACKRIDER FROM LOWNEY HANDY

Your letter just arrived.... You're just about god's gift to the artist colony. We were down to pennies. No fooling....

Willy [Lindsay] thinks he should go home. I think so too....

Now I've been planning to go back into the trailer—which Jim and I both hate heartily. Jim hates my messing things up—and I cook too much—from thwart. He's got it all shipshape—result of Army life—and I'm one of those badly trained Turners...Jim has had no youth. He needs a fling badly. There comes a time after you've worked for years when you are entitled. Most people take the fling first and they wake up middleaged with nothing much left...and that's what I wanted to prevent happening to you and Willy, you know all three of you had gotten off to a good start. But I wanted to sell you your writing — so good that the fling would be just a little vacation now and then. You'll be happier someday — although look at me come 46 in April — and I don't seem to have had either the fling or the work — although I suppose I've had credit more or less for both.

— Courtesy of Don Sackrider

[Lowney, James Jones, and Willard Lindsay were in California while Jones was completing From Here to Eternity. *The three were hard-pressed for funds, and Don, then in the Army, sent money to them. Tinks Howe was also supplying them cash when he could.—EDS.]*

EXTRACTS FROM A FEBRUARY 21, 1950, LETTER TO DON SACKRIDER FROM HARRY HANDY

Willy [Lindsay] is home, in case you didn't know. Arrived week ago Monday—tired, but not depressed. Haven't seen him since, but talked to him today and he's rested. His typewriter was due back from being repaired today, so he will, no doubt, get back to work. He is reported to get around some with Tinks [Howe]—a little burg & some chatter & he gets to know Robinson better to do the most of his book better. He should see our fair village with a different pair of eyes, see more behind what he sees.

Lowney says you want to put some of your cash into the deal to keep from spending it around. Well, I welcome your help greatly. The thing [the informal Handy Colony] has me almost on my back, right now. There were some extra expenses, particularly my vacation, and I'm paying income tax next month. So any help you want to give will be greatly, greatly appreciated.

I suggest that you make your first contribution to Willy. Say 25.00 a month. Keep track and Lowney will repay it as she still owes Willy

300.00. Then anymore you want to spare send to Jim—or balance it any way you want.

—*Courtesy of Don Sackrider*

[Tinks Howe knew a great deal about Robinson and its people, and Lowney was later to suggest to Jones that he talk frequently to his friend as he was gathering material for Some Came Running.—EDS.*]*

MARY ANN JONES

Mary Ann Jones, born in 1925, was the younger sister of James Jones. When their father committed suicide in 1942, she discovered his body; Mary Ann then went to live with their older brother and his family. For the next few years she lived with relatives, with a husband for a short while, with friends, and finally came to the Colony as the only female in late 1951.

Until October 1951 she was in Florida, and Lowney was sending instructions to her about her copying. Mary Ann's experience had been limited, and Lowney wanted her to dig more deeply within herself to find thoughts to express. As was always the case, she recommended certain authors to copy to help solve special problems. Mary Ann had started her novel, The Third Time You Killed Me, *but was still polishing her talent and developing her craft.*

In the archives of the University of Illinois at Springfield, there are two letters that Lowney wrote to Mary Ann. One was written in September 1951, shortly before Mary Ann came to the Colony, and the other in April 1952, when she was at the Colony and Lowney was in Florida. Both letters contained much personal information, as well as writing instructions. Because of this, excerpts from them are provided here as opposed to the entire letter. Lowney often wrote letters quickly, and her spelling, punctuation, and syntax were not always standard. Don notes that Lowney (and also Jim) sometimes deliberately used bad grammar to make a point. Don also remembers that Harry, in his slow, deliberate speech, would sometimes do the same.

EXTRACTS FROM A SEPTEMBER 3, 1951, LETTER TO MARY ANN JONES FROM LOWNEY HANDY

I was plumb puny when I last tried to write you and probably didn't make half sense with anything I said. I don't even recall what I wrote—so maybe I'd better run through a few things again—just in case.

Here's something I've discovered. Hemingway is usually thin for copying. Beyond getting the knack of doing dialogue, he don't offer much. But if you want perception, depth and really stuff for thinking and developing richness in your book—a novel with several layers is what they said of Jamie's [James Jones]—then I suggest that you slowly and carefully and THOUGHTFULLY copy Fitzgerald's Tender is *the Night*. It's in the Portable. If Fay took those when she left, you should buy yourself a set—HEMINGWAY, WOLFE, STEINBECK, FITZGERALD, FAULKNER—and copy these. Copy Mice a*nd Men* from Steinbeck and some from Faulkner—*The Bear*—is a good story. That should give you plenty for a while. I am positive you are really going to break them down next Spring. I'm betting on you with all I got. We've got to get some women writers to press.

And this will please you—I'm truly going good. Spent the last week here alone at Robinson (Harry was in New York) and I've finally found my stride. Truly, I'm hotter than a firecracker and it is truly DAMN GOOD. So lets form a pair of gold-dust twins and give them the double works come spring. Work hard. There's nothing pays off like steady consistently sticking to a job. It will put you in the front bracket.

—Courtesy of University of Illinois at Springfield Archives

EXTRACTS FROM AN APRIL 1, 1952, LETTER TO MARY ANN JONES FROM LOWNEY HANDY

You is doing swell. I can feel a change in the overall tone of your letter. Sent the book requested and think that now you'll get a lot out of it. NOTE WHAT THE AUTHOR SAYS.

Writing is a selection of detail—and the things you do not say are as important as the things you write. Good strong writing comes from this picture you have in mind. This is why I have you copy so much. I want you to get into your subconscious mind a jumble of all kinds of pictures and records. For EVERYTHING YOU COPY, SEE, HEAR,

THINK, OR EXPERIENCE BECOMES YOU. All you have to do is think about anything at all and it is part of you. Just thoughts. Thoughts make feelings, make cause and the cause leads to the result. There's a system to writing that is as mathematical as adding up 2+2+2 and getting 6. All the things I have you do are to get you to the final total.

The reason I told you to copy Ford Madox Ford (the conversational sections) is so you can get the feel of society fast talk or sophistication. Your own writing shows a tendency to talk too much like a teen-ager or like high school girls or even like waitresses. You will want to get another feel into your scenes when you do the parts with Olga. I have hunted here and there for things to do this. Try copying *The Sun Also Rises*. Get into the center of the book and copy conversations. Here's something else. Try and say (under your breath—but hear the spoken sound and rhythm of the sentences you copy) each sentence, so that you feel and hear what is being said and visualize the scene. BE SURE YOUR MIND IS COMPLETELY OCCUPIED WITH THE SCENES YOU COPY. Never work on anything if your mind wanders and there is even a hint of something on your mind besides your work, or something you thought about yesterday or you are worried about.

WORDS HAVE A POWER TO EXPRESS THE AUTHORITY BEHIND THEM. They are your tools. They are your material. Although they seemingly are an abstraction, they become solid as concrete and as hard hitting as a ball bat if you have a feeling in your own mind. For anyone who feels strongly conveys his emotions. The feeling always comes through the words. So always know exactly what you want to say. Get the mind busy with the overall effect; what emotion do you want your reader to have—do you want him to be angry or glad or upset or joyous. Don't plan how to say what you want to say— BUT THE EFFECT YOU WANT TO LEAVE. The strength lies in knowing what you feel. If you try to choose words to leave a planned effect it goes wide of the mark. But if you hold an emotion inside you, the words seem to fall into pattern and the needed expressions just come of themselves. It is your subconscious rising into the reasoning conscious mind and giving it the tools to do the most effective work. BUT FIRST YOU HAVE TO GIVE THE SUBCONSCIOUS MIND THE MATERIALS—they have to be there on file. Then the little brownies hunt the right one out and hand it to your conscious mind and bang!—I write a letter with strength and you get the emotion out of the letter that may or may not lie between the lines. You get a hazy picture from the emotion in my mind.

Remember idle words are empty words; they contain no reality, for there is no thought, no feeling, no emotion behind them. Words cannot convey what is not in the mind. Remember it is very, very important to see a picture—and learn to hold the picture or the anger or the sorrow or some overall feeling in your mind. And always know what the emotion is that you plan to leave with your readers. You can see why I have put you on a study of learning words. Making lists and learning their meaning. You have to memorize them so that you can use them easily and without thought of the conscious mind—the use will come from the subconscious mind where you will have them stored—along with scraps of scenes and a million usable things from the copying and living and thinking and all of it is jumbled together— that makes you an individual different from all others in existence. In getting the lists of words and learning them so they are part of you, you are becoming a brain—the only way they can test your IQ is by finding out how many words you can use and understand so that you know their full meaning and use. If you don't know the word, oblivious, you don't know the action that you have when you blank out. If you don't know the word you don't have all the words you could use to express lost in thought—or a million miles away—which is a slang expression. But the word oblivious tells it in one word. You see, good writing is a selection of detail.

If I write as the opening sentence to a novel or story, "The Gulf was a pond, the soft slow waves washed the edge of the beach." Or if I write, "The grey sullen waves were heavy and coated with oil, their leaden peaks were lethal and threatened to crush the boat within their hungry arms." I've used a picture in my mind to set the emotion for an entirely different story. The Gulf may be dirty and none of these—it may not even look inviting for swimming or even a walk alongside, but I go into my mind—VISUALIZE—and see a Gulf of my own that becomes more real than the real one and I set the pace (THE EMO-TIONAL FEEL IN THE MIND OF THE READER) for my story.

In fact, my Gulf may be put into a South Sea's island—and it is no longer the Gulf of Mexico—in fact it may be surrounded by mountains. But first you must know what mountains look like and than you send down to your subconscious mind for what you have stored in the encyclopedic files. Now it may be that you have never seen a mountain—only in movies and painted pictures and in photographs and read about them by someone who loves mountains—good poetry—and good description is all you need. If you know yourself, have a good library and can think at all, you can write about anything. Experience is yours for the taking. You don't have to live each and every experience—you just have to be able to see it and think about it, for anything you visualize is your own. Christ said, "Any man who has looked at a woman with adultery in his mind has already committed adultery." The same is true of writing—what you read and store is your own for the Bible also says "THERE IS NOTHING NEW UNDER THE SUN." The originality comes from the way you put things together and from the selection of detail you have filed in your subconscious.

I suggest that you broaden your reading. Have you read Conrad? I suggest that you read this Ford Madox Ford book—although I heartily disagree with his interpretation of females—but in reading it, it may annoy you so much that you can do a better scene—about something you feel is not represented as it should be.

You don't need to worry about being financed—at all—either Jim or I both will carry you. I will let you know in plenty of time before I come out so you can just relax and go into all you stuff you can get stored. LEARN WORDS. SEE MOVIES. ALWAYS THINK AND FEEL AND STORE IT for the book Nothing is wasted in writing. Everything is grist for the mill—and everything works out—just you mind (you have three levels of mind-force) at work, and gradually with the system that I am teaching you—you will learn to co-ordinate all three of your minds and then GENIUS..THAT IS THE SYSTEM.

Love to you, Always

—Courtesy of University of Illinois at Springfield Archives

It is clear that Lowney felt Mary Ann would achieve much and be-
come a writer. Mary Ann Jones died suddenly in June of 1952 at the
Handy Colony at Marshall, Illinois. Her novel, The Third Time You Killed
Me, *was never finished nor was it ever submitted to a publisher. The*
novel indicates a talent worth nourishing and an ability worth cultivat-
ing. The characters in the book are well developed and delineated. The
scenes and events are easy to believe and very appropriate for the period.
There is some coincidence but it is not used to excess, as is so often the
case in young writers. Although the novel wasn't finished, it is hard to see
how the ending could possibly include "They lived happily ever after."

SYNOPSIS OF

THE THIRD TIME YOU KILLED ME

The novel deals with life as seen by a young woman, Martha
Lawrence. It tells of the problems she has faced and continues to face
and her attempts to escape and find a better life. It seems that every
accomplishment requires much effort.

Martha is twenty years old and has completed one year of college in
the small town where she lives with her aunt, Agatha Lawrence. The
college is a religious school and primarily trains young men for the min-
istry. Aunt Agatha is very strict and has many rules that Martha must
obey: no makeup, no smoking, home by midnight. She is permitted to date the
young men from the school if Agatha has met and approved of them.

Martha has been raised by her aunt who was the only sister of her
father, Fred Lawrence.

Fred was killed before Martha was born. Fred had lived with his
sister in their family home, which belonged to Fred, prior to his marriage. After he and Maria were married they continued to live there.
Because she was pregnant, Maria continued this arrangement after
Fred's death even though Agatha treated her quite badly and considered her inferior to the Lawrence family, both morally and socially. After
Martha's birth, Maria's life became even more impossible and in des-

peration she finally left, leaving the child behind. This is not clearly explained in the book but, in time, Agatha somehow gains legal custody of Martha and also complete control of Fred's estate. Martha has an interest in the property, but she appears not to be aware of it for a long time.

Through the years Agatha has filled Martha's head with only bad stories about her mother and wonderful tales of her father. Martha believes that her mother abandoned her because she did not love her and did not want her as part of her life. She has never heard from her mother nor had any contact with her, but it appears this might be Agatha's doing. The effect on the young woman is profound. Shortly before the end of her first year of college she meets someone who changes everything.

This is when Martha meets Olga Feathers, an old and dear friend of her mother and also a friend of her father. She now hears for the first time the truth about her family. Olga and her husband, Carl, live in California where Carl is a pilot in the Navy. They are a childless couple, and Olga is very taken with the young woman. She is furious over the lies Martha has been told about her mother and also the way her aunt has manipulated and completely controls Martha's life. When she asks Martha to come to California and live with her and Carl, Martha thinks this may be the answer to all of her problems. After an ugly and final confrontation with her aunt, Martha leaves for California.

The novel then deals with the people Martha meets, the friends of Olga and Carl, the young men who work with Carl, the people with whom Martha works, the young men who become a part of her life, and the lasting effect all of these have. Martha is very naive, and she is not the best judge of character in many cases. She has many problems, some of which she is able to solve and some which even solve themselves. Olga does not prove to be the most stable character for Martha to emulate, but they remain friends. Martha finally becomes involved with Jimmy, a young sailor she meets when out with friends, and they appear to be trying to establish a life together.

The end of Chapter 11 is obviously not the end of the story, but only the end of what has been written. One cannot help but wonder what the rest would have contained. How would the author have solved the problems, and who would have been the victor at the close? As mentioned earlier, there is no way they ALL could have lived happily ever after.

JOHN BOWERS

EXTRACTS FROM A DECEMBER 16, 1962, LETTER TO JOHN BOWERS FROM LOWNEY HANDY

I believe in telepathy, although I don't know the how and whys of it, but about a week before you wrote me, you kept coming into my mind and I told someone (Harry was listening too) all about your book, your brother, your war, you going to school in Canada.... I was telling them about taking your book to Random House, and how I all but got it published....

[O]nce I went in to the MCA office and collected (OR RATHER TRIED TO COLLECT) 8 manuscript novels—remember I took 8 in with me the time I took your book in—eight seems to be a number that haunts me—and I got six of them back—one book that was terrific and loaded with the best slang I ever saw—VERY ORIGINAL—is still missing—they claim they lost it in the mail—MEN GO HALVES—by William Duhart. He sold several things—and then last winter—Bill had been sending me some yellow magazines he was publishing in—Bill was raping his manuscript—he had a carbon—and using stuff from it—JIM ALSO DID THIS TO HIS FIRST NOVEL THEY SHALL INHERIT THE LAUGHTER—he had a lot of good stuff in it—but most of it has been used I believe—I have a copy of LAUGHTER—but haven't looked at it.

I have a copy of so much—like REX BOLIN's HALF RED MAN. Rex wrote three books—and can't place them—Howard Pehrson wrote three and can't sell them....

There is so much I just can't tell you. I don't have the strength to do what I used to do—I had a stroke last winter—not a bad one but a warning—and the doctor said I just had to cut down on my work. Where I used to write to anyone who wrote to me—and try hard to get them to write and sell—today I am not doing that—I am picking my people.

You know I don't know a thing about you—your age—THIS IS IMPORTANT—life runs in cycles of every seven years, and you change and have peaks at certain times. WHEN WERE YOU BORN—

under what zodiacal constellation—this is important—because I usually group these people to work with—NOT PHYSICALLY—but mentally—and I group them for their tie-in with forces and energies—FORCES ARE PLANETARY AND LUNAR (the past) and Solar is Energies—mental, the soul is son-of-mind....

You know I used to love history and read it all the time—I liked particularly the German writer Feuchtwanger—and read him avidly—today I can't read him because his technique is bad. I'm a fanatic on technique—and have really learned a lot since you were there. Maybe its because my vibrations are higher. YOU KNOW WE ARE COMING INTO A NEW AGE OF WRITING—and all creative arts....

I will write you more later—am very very tired...and I do have to watch out that I don't over work.

I can teach you to take my place, if you like....

Love, ever,

—Courtesy of John Bowers

This story is set in the early fifties during the same period the Handy Colony flourished. In comparison with today's climate, it was a period of repression—culturally, emotionally and sexually. My original title was "Explosives," which may be taken metaphorically or literally. People worked at an explosive factory. They were explosive inside, for when you dam up things inside, they sometimes explode outside. We were free at the Colony to discuss so many things that weren't common coin in the rest of the country. The beatniks and Kerouac hadn't arrived and the Hippie was far down the horizon. We knew so much and so little at the Colony. I brought up Henry Miller once to Jim and he had never heard of him. I was hesitant, and with reason, not to bring him up with Lowney. I don't think she would have appreciated his male rambunctiousness and picaresque sexual capers. We were brought into another time zone at the Colony, and it was not Plato's Republic. I've been tinkering with this story for some time. I even added a few lines to the ending in the last week. I'll probably keep doing so ad infinitum. I have a collection of stories, of which this

one is included, called Love in Tennessee, which explores the variety of love in that place and time from which I sprang. I hope to get the collection published some day. Lowney didn't get to put her pencil to this story, but the emotional content is from her period in my life.
—John Bowers

LONG GONE IN TENNESSEE

By John Bowers

I heard about it in the barbershop. They were hiring over in Kingeport, some kind of ordinary job anyone could do, some kind of clerk's job. It was in a new plant that produced a mysterious something. They had a lot of plants like that in East Tennessee. We had never known—or cared—what they made in these plants. They had once made something at Oak Ridge and few gave it a second thought. You just accepted whatever it was—cars, films, bloomers or bombs. It was all the same. It was just another thing you accepted—like playing football when you were a kid, playing hurt, getting baptized, and going into the Armed Services when you turned eighteen. Taken for granted. Never questioned. There were other more important things. Like whether or not you were ever going to get laid.

I was hired as a timekeeper in Payroll. I sat in a large room at a desk with an adding machine before me and many desks around me. I took time sheets, added up the time and the pay, deducted tax and Social Security, and turned it over for a supervisor's scrutiny, and then someone down the line made out pay checks. It was cut and dry, and before long I could do it in sleep. And I was soon near to being asleep through the day. Our shift started at seven in the morning and ended at four in the afternoon. I never found out why we started so early, but then the whole operation was a little peculiar. Whatever was actually made at the plant must have been a doozy, something that might go off any minute with a tremendous bang because smoking or lighting a match was heavily restricted. Big red warning signs were everywhere, and we had to take smokes in a small, nearly airtight chamber, with the roominess of a submarine, where a fog became as dense as in a steam bath.

Misfits of one kind or another worked at the plant. No self-respecting, average, totally sane person would have considered it. I was a misfit. I had traveled a bit, and had come back to town not sure what my next move would be. I wasn't trained to do anything. Certain Tennesseans from Appalachia travel from time to time—to Detroit, Chicago, and L.A. You learn some big city ways but you miss certain things, something as simple as cornbread, and you come back. But you can't fit in the way you used to and you become a misfit. You go to work at a place like the plant, rolling out of bed at five, wolfing down a quick breakfast your mother gets up to make for you because a mother can love even a misfit, and you wait in a comatose state for headlights to glow suddenly outside your house, the signal that your car pool of fellow misfits has arrived. It took about an hour to get to the plant.

Cocky Cox drove. He had been a couple of years ahead of me in school. He had a blond crew cut, always had, even, I remember, when we played against each other in Midget Summer Softball and when, most spectacularly, he had been star quarterback and point guard in high school. He kept his hair the way he always had. Nature would have to do something about it. He wouldn't. He was a traditionalist. Old timers still talked about some of the games he had almost single-handedly won. There was always blood on his jersey. Practically my only memories of him back then were of someone on a green grass field or a lacquered court. I have no memory of him in a classroom. I see him now, dribbling downcourt on a shiny waxed floor, how all was quiet except for the squeak of sneakers, all eyes on Cocky. Once he pressed a finger against a nostril and blew a wad out the other. Right on court. It was a pretty crude macho thing to do, and any other guy would have received a lot of hoots. Not Cocky. Back then he could get away with anything, do anything. Or so we thought. He got married his senior year and that was really something. No one ever did that in high school. His wife was a year older, and I remember her sitting in the stands watching him play in a tournament. She had one of those terrific athletic builds you could die for. Her calves were as muscular as his. She was smiling. Her teeth had the whiteness of milk. Cocky never went to college. He could be counted on for a joke or two on the drive over, but they invariably fell flat and he would sink into gloom. He was a cautious driver.

Walter Pat would be nervously seated in the backseat as I climbed in beside him. He always had a ready smile, a wave of his hand: Always a great crease to his trousers, which he had a habit of running his fingers down, and his dark hair was carefully slicked back in a neat pompadour. Walter Pat had a superior-sounding title at the plant; he was called an accountant. He never pursued women like the rest of us—fine, we thought, more for us; except no one was getting any anyhow. He lived with his mother in a small apartment. He never invited any of us there. Up front, by Cocky, sat Hawk who was part Indian—a large part—and, like Cocky, married. We never said anyone was happily married or unhappily. They were just married. It was hard for Hawk to laugh. I'm not sure he could. Whenever he heard or said anything funny wind came out of his mouth in a grunt and his eyes widened. That's what passed for a laugh. He had married a girl who, the story went, was in love with someone else. She was pretty sexy so I could understand why Hawk could be led into matrimony— that, and the fact that he had knocked her up. At least someone had.

Fern Johanson, secretary to the superintendent of the plant, was the last to swing in. She had a pretty high position for a misfit. She came down the walk from her house the moment we pulled up, our headlights cutting the dark. She held a cigarette between her lips, a thumb hooked defiantly under the strap of her shoulder bag, and she flicked her cigarette away in a high red arc just before stretching a long, nyloned leg in the car to claim space between Walter and me. "Hi, boys, how you doing?" We passed few cars on the curvy road to Kingeport. The tires hummed, the car swayed, and no one said much. I scrunched down, still missing my bed. Walter Pat kept straightening his pant creases. Cocky and Hawk looked ahead as the highway unfolded.

One morning something amazing happened. Truly amazing. With no preliminaries, Fern suddenly pulled up her sweater, reached back, unclasped her bra, and shook two large titties back and forth. "How do you like them babies, boys?" she said. I woke up. Walter Pat began straightening his pant creases frantically. I knew there was no dance card here to sign, no guidelines, but something should follow her display or her feelings might be hurt, as her hands went languidly behind her head. Also it was sort of exciting, the truth be known. I held one breast, then the other. I felt her nipples between my fingers turn hard. I began sucking first one and then the other, both of us scrunching as far down as possible so Hawk and Cocky wouldn't notice. Somehow Walter Pat didn't count. We drove into the plant's parking lot, and Hawk said, "Well, shit, another fucking day." And so, straightening up, bra hook fastened, sweater down, Fern and the rest of us trudged in the plant to pass through metal detectors before assuming our places behind desks.

Fern never took the ride back with us and we only saw her in the mornings in the dark. Her boss kept her overtime on the other side of the building, and at night she hung out with the older set of ne'er-do-wells of the town, and there was never a steady boyfriend. That was the way she wanted it. Gladiola Jenkins took Fern's place on the drive back. Her dark luxuriant hair was pulled back in a prim bun, and her narrow face was perpetually set in a display of disapproval. Her mouth was frequently puckered, too, as if she had just tasted a lemon. We learned quickly that she was Pentecostal, for she no more than settled back than she gave us bulletins on river water baptisms, camp meetings, and revivals coming up. Just what we wanted to hear. She wore no lipstick, she wore no rouge. The perfume that emanated from her strongly was not from a bottle but a self-produced musk. It was so powerful that every time she crossed her sturdy legs all heads perked up. An animal in heat had just entered. She told us proudly that she was getting married to an elder in the church. Hawk couldn't restrain himself. "You let him have any yet?"

Her face instantly took on ugly red blotches. "I ought to slap your smarty face," she yelled. "You're not going to talk dirty to me in this car. I'm going to report you to the plant supervisor if you ever try it again. I'll get you fired."

That should have quieted Hawk. It certainly would have me. Hawk kept going. He kept going with mock seriousness. "I'm sorry, Gladiola. I didn't mean to get out of line. I take it back. You've kissed him, haven't you?"

"No, we've never kissed. No man has ever kissed me or ever will before we're married. Marriage is sacred and its vows are that you come to it pure and unsoiled. I could never go into marriage if I came into it impure."

"What about your intended?" Hawk couldn't stop putting her on because he thought probably she was putting him on. "You going to let him get by with having kissed someone before?"

Cows grazed in fields to the side of us. The sun blazed down. We'd put in a full day and barely had enough energy to get interested in Gladiola's romantic life. "He's never kissed anybody either."

"Well, I wish you both the very best of luck," Hawk said in an exaggerated manner. Then he let his breath out sharply between his teeth, his eyes brightening, his way of laughing.

We drank beer at night to revive our spirits, to not throw in the towel and return to bed without celebration. Beer made us think once more of girls, of women, of sex. It might have been all we thought about. Through the day in payroll we'd spent our time socializing, telling jokes and turning most everything into double entendres. There were married men and women in payroll, but never with spouses together. None had a good word to say for his or her absent partner. None. "She don't do nothing but nag," a man might say. "Lays about all day and then gets to work on me when I get home. Do this, do that." From a woman: "God, he's driving me crazy. Wants me to cook his dinner, wash his socks, do everything in the house, and he can't get it through his thick skull that I've put in a full day like him. He only wants to listen to ball scores and then go to sleep." Everyone was horny, man and woman. And no one seemed to know what to do about it. It was building up in all of us. It felt as if it might explode at any minute, like the plant. No misfit thought of love as the answer. Love was something that had happened in the past, something to mourn over, cry over, and have regrets about, something to listen to people sing about on the jukebox. It was something you might consider for the future, but nothing that you thought you deserved today.

One night, Hawk said to me over a beer in the Varsity Grill: "I know some girls who'll put out for us. I've got my car. You interested?"

It was a given among our crowd that married men carried on the same as single men—maybe more so because marital restrictions only made them more desperate. "I'm interested. Who?"

"Two who live near me. I'll call, but you got to go in and pick them up."

"Why me?"

"Their people know I'm married, but it's a cinch for you. Just knock on their door, and if you get asked about anything, say you're giving them a lift somewhere. Something like that. Everybody will understand, but you got to go through the formalities."

Hawk made the call on the wall phone at the Varsity. Music was blaring on the jukebox and pool balls clicked. He was shouting into the phone. "Let's roll, buddy," he said, hanging up. "They're ready."

I knocked on the front door of a large, white-frame house, my hands sweating, and a woman in an apron waved me in. Inside a lot of action was going on: a baby crawling around in diapers; old folk sitting in easy chairs; a strong-looking man in green work clothes reading a paper; some people playing cards at the dining room table. I was glad to enter into such a large family setting. It was less scary somehow. The TV was on low. A phonograph blasted away out of sight. I felt guilty, yet excited. I couldn't keep an idiot grin off my face. Before I could go into any rigmarole, the woman in the apron yelled up the stairs, "Anita, Jackie! That boy you were expecting is here!" My intricate story of how I was going to take the girls for tryouts at the Little Theater was not needed. Also, I was not exactly a boy. Then I saw a blur of forms descend the stairs in a wreath of talcum, shampoo, and soap, and head past me right out the door. Neither one of the two girls gave any indication that I was there. I might have been invisible. One was slightly taller than the other. Both were knockouts. Old Hawk. I followed behind.

Anita, the taller one, got in front beside Hawk. Jackie hesitated a moment, then got in the backseat beside me. "Boy, am I glad to get out tonight! BOR-ing!" Anita said, snuggling over beside Hawk. "You're the awfulest old thing, though. If some man ever did to me what you're doing to Little Bit, I'd kill him."

"My wife knows I have to have a little fun on the side or I'd be hell to live with, but anything you say."

Ten minutes before I'd been drinking beer in the Varsity Grill. Now I was actually sitting beside a real live female, not dreaming about it, one who smelled like a bar of soap, who had hair the color of caramel, someone who wore a white, starched blouse and a tight pair of shorts even though it was getting into fall. She had terrific legs, too, tanned nut brown. This was Jackie. "What do you do?" I said.

"Oh, this and that." She seemed on edge, distracted.

"I mean, are you in college or working or what?"

"Hey," she said, not answering, putting her arms on the seat behind Hawk: "I saw you at the Majestic the other night, Hawk. You stuck up old thing, you didn't even speak."

"I go to the Majestic to see movies, not socialize."

Hawk decided that we should go to the lake near the Erwin fish hatchery. "Let's take in some scenery," was how he put it. Deep trees lined it and only a vague outline of it showed from where we parked on a white graveled lot. Moonlight washed over us and the air was sweet and slightly cool. "Anita and I are going to take a stroll," Hawk announced. "We'll be back in about a half hour. Don't do anything I wouldn't do."

"Wait a minute," Anita said. "Don't I get asked or something?"

"Okay, would you like to stroll down lover's lane *avec moi*?" Hawk said in an exaggerated way. He had been to college for a couple of semesters and thought he could get away with fancy talk when he was with a girl.

"Just stop taking me for granted," Anita said.

"And don't be too long," Jackie said.

"I never am," said Hawk.

Then Jackie and I were alone. Now what? The first thing to do was get nervous. "Well?" she said, moving away from me, frowning. "Well," I said, preparing to become angry because I foresaw her keeping her legs pressed together, moving my roving hand away. Frankly it would have been a relief if she had. All of this was getting just too dramatic. Instead, she didn't turn her head when I bent near, but still she frowned. Then it hit both of us that we possibly might, we possibly might just do it. We acknowledged the moment, like partners before a dance. We went into another mode. At first Jackie feigned distaste, uncomfortableness, a semblance of fright. But some deep compulsion, deeper than our bones, pressed us forward. A gun to my head wouldn't have stopped me. We kissed, like saying hello, and then here came her brassiere being unfastened—wow! She was no longer frowning, and she slid out of her shorts and snow-white underpants. I was lowering my trousers. "Come on," she said. Come on, I did, although I wasn't used to such encouragement. Usually I had to fight for every inch of ground, like a soldier at Guadalcanal. I knew my time was short, too, so I grabbed, sucked, and thrust like a man just out of prison—which, in a way, I was. The Lord knows what I had released in her. She clawed my back, rode her legs up me, and whispered endearments as if she were coaxing a horse down the stretch. Suddenly, she came to her senses and said, "Don't you go shooting anything in me!" I didn't. I thrust love's arrow into Hawk's upholstery. We lay still a moment as if a St. Vitas dance, or a freight train, had just passed through us. Then she slipped back into her clothes in the blink of an eye and said, "Now look what you've gone and done made me do." *Me*?

I didn't know what to say, so I did an amazing thing. I went for a swim in the buff, right there in the lake, in October, at the Fish Hatchery. The water wasn't that cold once you got over the first heart-stopping moment, and I swam underwater, the total darkness and unreality exhilarating. I came out, wiping the lake water off, then holding my arms together, hopping on the gravel in the moonlight. I put on my clothes and shivered in the backseat. Everyone looked at me as if I was crazy. Maybe I was. Hawk drove the girls straight back to their house—not much time for any conversation, no time for a drive-in snack. Nothing. Jackie did not offer her lips in parting, but simply raised her hand, stepped out, and then was swallowed up, along with Anita, in the large, white-frame house, where the people were moving around as if nothing had happened. Hawk said, "How'd you do?"

"Well, okay," I said, a little uncomfortably.

"I've got to tell you something."

"Now what?"

"She's only thirteen."

"Thirteen!"

"She's a little advanced, ain't she?"

"Advanced? She's like a full-grown woman! Thirteen!"

"Ain't that something?"

Oh God, there are some things worse than being a misfit. There's being a felon, a criminal, and a miserable cur. I couldn't sleep that night, and sadly remembered how sleepy I'd been early that evening. I remembered those innocent beers I'd had. I thought of Jackie, and I thought of that white-frame home, and I beat my head against the mattress. Hawk wanted everybody in trouble. Hawk was wretched at home, and he wanted everyone else miserable. Hawk had signed my death warrant.

I could carry on no conversation in the car pool. Fern Johanson could pull her titties out to a faretheewell, I was not interested. I looked at a row of figures and saw a row of bars. At the boarding house where I sometimes ate, a deputy sheriff also ate. I couldn't keep my eyes off his holster and forty-five and the way the bullets gleamed in the sockets on his wide belt. I had trouble passing the biscuits, had trouble understanding words and questions. Thirteen! I couldn't put a rational thought together. Done for. I kept away from Hawk. I stopped drinking beer. All Jackie had to do is to spread the word and I'm electrocuted.

Nothing happened for a month, no knock on the door, no call from the police. Slowly I began to relax. I decided to take in a movie. No sooner had I stepped in the Majestic than, of course, there she stood by the popcorn machine, sipping a Coke, towering over some girls around her. I tried to convince myself she looked twenty-five, but that was hard to do. She was giggling and throwing her hands around, and she wore saddle-oxfords. Our eyes met and hers got big. I thought, dear God, she's going to scream. She didn't. She gave me the tiniest wave, turned, and disappeared into the dark cavern of the theater. I took the opposite aisle, and, wouldn't you know, there sat Hawk, who, seeing me alone, patted an empty seat beside him.

Little cliques of girls and guys were scattered through the theater, all with their individual style of appreciating the fare. A fat boy went "me-ow" everytime an actress came on screen, and hoots followed. Someone threw popcorn. Swoons came from girls when a Hollywood handsome man came on. I wanted very much to talk to Hawk, but he had other things on his mind. He was in a trance. He leaned forward, his mouth slightly open. I poked him with my elbow. "Hawk, listen. Hawk—"

"Shsss! Shsss! I want to watch!"

Donald Duck was on screen, and Hawk was making that soundless laugh. I leaned back into the past, back to where shards of memory live, back to where it's all over and nothing can change a thing, back to wonder whether you're a misfit or fit in all too well, back to wonder what shards of memory others may carry of the same events.

JOHN BOWERS

Extracts from a January 7, 1963, letter
to John Bowers from Lowney Handy

Your trouble as ALWAYS is still living in the past—CHRIST SAID, "Let the dead past bury its dead."

You need to think about that a lot. It is astonishing how much your letter is involved with the past.

I can't remember what Norm [Mailer] looks like—and think he is nuts—I'd not want to be closer than 200 miles of him or anyone else you mention....

Do you think I recall anyone who was even in the camp...not a soul. If I had to give a remembered picture of James Jones to the cops— I sure as hell couldn't do it.

That was another life.

THE HANDY COLONY IS NO MORE. I died.

Now see if you can write.

We can never work worth two cents until we get free of our personality—stop chit-chatting—intellectualizing.

That is not working—not being a writer.

You are an intellectual.

I doubt if you'll write.

BECAUSE YOU ARE OF THE PERSONALITY. You don't forget life around you—the past—all the silly things you muddle over. Maybe you'll sell stuff...so what. I WANT THE BEST WRITERS IN THE MARKET—and when they stop being it—I look for someone else.

This is the key to success. I have no sentimentality.

I've been married to Harry Handy since July 1926...simply because he works—DID I TELL YOU HE HAS A BOOK ABOUT READY FOR PUBLICATION—and it is no slouch—at 56 he decided he didn't want to be with the oil business anymore—so he became a writer....

Good luck to you John—I wish you the best—I have loved you in my way—because I think I knew you in other lives. You have a problem. BUT YOU ALSO KNOW HOW TO SOLVE IT—They say, if you throw enough shit some of it sticks.—and I'm sure you know the ropes by now.

71

So if you write—or don't isn't up to me—BUT YOU.

and the handy colony went down the drain with jones—Chamales died almost 3 years ago—he'd had it—Success had ruined Rock Hudson. I wouldn't buy all the others EVEN IF THEY DO PUBLISH—that was at the colony—for 15¢ at a sale.

Jim's wife (gloria—he used to call her Moss—then Mos) once said to me—Lowney you can't let Jim go—he's the best writer you ever had. And I said I don't know—Time will prove that.

Today I'm still looking for the best writers—and time is still on my side.

Love and kisses.

—Courtesy of John Bowers

HARRY HANDY

Harry Handy wrote his novel, Turnaround, *after he had retired and moved to the Colony. It has never been published, but it contains much worthwhile material. Many of the characters need more development, and sometimes it seems there are far too many included.*

Lowney's correspondence contains a February 7, 1950, letter from Scribner's Burroughs Mitchell concerning her novel, But Answer Came There None. *The critique he makes of her novel could also apply to Harry's in many ways. This is what he said:*

"There is good writing in these chapters, and there are interesting things said. I'd expect that from you. But I cannot feel that your plan for the development of suspense is working out. For me at least the suspense and the mystery aren't sufficiently there; I don't believe the reader is going to stay with you to find out who is murdered and who is guilty. Somehow the suspense doesn't mount as it should. I am sure you have planned out your story very carefully, but I have to say that the effect *of its design seems rather helter-skelter. Your people are sharply described, your observations on the town are shrewd and telling; but something—perhaps it's the underlying plan—prevents these characters from coming close to the reader. He isn't made to care about them." (Courtesy of University of Illinois at Springfield Archives)*

Harry also fails to develop the suspense sufficiently to bring his reader into the action. One finds that the interest simply isn't there. By the time he reaches the denouement, he simply finds a niche in which to place the characters without having even hinted that this was to occur. Certainly an editor could have fixed many of these problems had the novel reached that stage. Unfortunately, his death precluded that.

The novel covers a two-week period during which the chemical plant undergoes a "turnaround." This term describes a period during which the entire plant is shut down for full maintenance on all units and for installing any new equipment. Because all production stops, it is necessary that this be done in the shortest possible time.

The novel begins without introduction to Barney Ranger, operating superintendent for Roanoke Chemicals, Inc., and his wife, Hazel. Their relationship, attitudes and individuality are established, as well as their place in the social structure of the community. Chapter 2 deals with the "turnaround" itself and is a perfect example of Handy's ability as a writer.
—Helen Howe

TURNAROUND

By Harry Handy

2

Closing the door on his comfortable living room Barney Ranger glanced sharply at the threatening clouds, then with one continuous motion, he slid into his white Chevy pickup, pulling the door shut, and started the motor.

He turned on the headlights and backed out of the carport, stones rattling as he hit the street, and mushed off through a layer of loose gravel, hoping the city would not take all summer laying an asphalt surface. He skidded around the corner and came to a rolling stop at State Road 11, turning left, gunned the company-owned Chevy down the long slope toward Albany; the tenseness he had felt since before leaving home was beginning to subside.

Suddenly it occurred to him that Hazel had seemed more than a little edgy all evening and had flared up unreasonably over this trouble-shooting call. Now he wondered if in some way she had gotten a hint of his new girlfriend at French Lick. Or even of Doris Monroe in the executive offices over in Louisville.

If it came to the worst, he decided, he might be able to explain green-eyed Doris Monroe last winter. Then he had spent three days conferring at Roanoke headquarters. Doris was a very smart and clever girl, and he might be able to account for taking such an interest. She had quietly tipped him off that the home office was beginning to wonder about Roanoke public relations in Albany. Yes, that story just might go over with Hazel, since Doris had implied that top-man Doctor Paul Brossard had complete confidence in Barney Ranger.

But it would hardly account for Marlene Atkins up at the French Lick Inn. Another matter entirely, for if Hazel found out about that tall blonde, Marlene would turn out to be dynamite. He scowled, then fatalistically shrugged it away, to concentrate on that balky third boiler which had to be on the line tonight.

It was hard to explain to Hazel how his chemical plant could not run with only two boilers. And how it was impossible to shut down properly without having all three of these boilers on the line; she was convinced that all he had to do was simply put out the furnace fires.

But if that damn third boiler was not running, his whole goddamn program for shutting down was completely fouled up. Before they got the boiler on, the feed-water pump had to work; Power Foreman Larson insisted he couldn't make it go at all.

Barney hit the gas pedal. Well, they couldn't make steam without water in the boiler. Sure as hell the tubes would burn up, and there would be an explosion. Then, by God, they would really be up the creek.

He yanked the pickup back over the centerline, trying to figure why that goddamn pump governor was tripping ahead of time. Only last week he and Scott Larson had checked it out okay, and now Larson said the son of a bitch tripped off even before the machine got up to its normal thirty-six hundred revolutions-per-minute. How the hell this could be, he couldn't for the life of him figure. And on Friday night, too. Christ Almighty, always right on the goddamn nose! With turn-around commencing Monday.

A gust of wind from the deserted parking lot assaulted the light pickup, specking the windshield with a trace of rain. He switched on the wipers.

It was a goddamn vicious circle. Tomorrow at noon he'd ordered the hydrocracker furnace fires to be cut. No longer would there be hot flue gas. The waste-heat steam generators would go dead. At the same time the steam demand in other sections of the plant would rise way above normal, at least half the capacity of the boiler Larson was trying to get started. It was a damn cinch he had to have steam enough to get everything shut down safely after tomorrow noon.

He flicked off the wipers, hearing his tires sucking at the wet asphalt, and again checked over his schedule in his mind. Throughout the coming two weeks every piece of equipment was to undergo a vigorous inspection. Monday morning ninety extra men were to report in, all of them mechanics that Baxter Brothers had contracted to supply.

Even the tools they would need had already been checked out and were on the job. And if Roanoke processing equipment was not down (oil and gas free, and cool), these extra mechanics would not have a damn thing to do.

Ninety men standing around waiting would soon run up a hell of a lot of extra cost. To say nothing of shooting his time schedule full of holes. Christ! They had to be ready to go.

He gave the horn to a jalopy and rolled by the Plaza in the center of town, passing one of Al Kruger's big vans to make the green light at the Albany House corner.

Barney noted the new tractor pulling the van and thought how Kruger must be doing all right since his plant was organized. Suddenly he remembered Manager Roger Slocum's instructions for him, to try and find out how the hell the A.F. of L. had sneaked up on Kruger Tile overnight.

Whipping across U.S. 60 on the yellow with horns blasting, he skimmed by a taxi in front of Harlan Bradley's new liquor store. At Roanoke Avenue he turned west toward the plant, only half-seeing the lighted houses and cars parked at the curb. The wide streets were empty of moving traffic, and through new maple leaves he could now see the plant lights and a white plume blasting off the battery of boilers.

He rolled down his window for a better look, and for the first time heard the ripping tearing racket of blasting steam. It carried clear across town. The roar completely dominated the soothing hum of ordinary plant operation, and in two seconds he identified the source of the blast, the hand-operated bleed valve on No. 3 boiler had been wheeled wide open, a dead giveaway that Scott Larson had fired up the boiler too damn fast.

Already too goddamn hot. Goddamn! He glared at the blasting steam. Without that trip-happy feed pump Larson didn't have the water pumping capacity to risk putting No. 3 in the header. Larson should have checked out that pump today. Before he even lighted off the fire.

This wasn't the first time Scott Larson had been too damn ambitious, always itching to jump into a program. And then Larson would start yelling for help when he got into a jam. Yet his men liked him: Barney's eyes grew stormy.

He coasted around the circular island which ended the avenue laid out midway between Roanoke's main office and their floodlighted chemical plant. His headlights picked up the inclined plate-glass walls of the gatehouse.

The slat-roofed building bore a striking resemblance to an airport control tower. The burly guard had been alerted by his headlights. Barney watched Bill Gagin set his uniform hat firmly on his graying head, then limp out of the gatehouse and throw a powerful flashlight beam into the pickup.

"It's me," he yelled above the blasting steam. "I'm going down to the boilers, Bill, if anyone wants me."

Gagin stepped over to peer inside the cab. "Throw that damn cigarette away," he growled. Then he turned off his flashlight and hobbled back into the gatehouse where he held down a button. The chain-link gate slid open. Behind him Barney noted the heavy frame glide back shut tight as he rolled on between two towering white structures and came out in the center of the floodlighted plant.

He turned left, his headlights sweeping the windows of his own office occupying one end of the substantial one-story plant office building and ran past the brick control house to skirt the solvent plant. He pulled in beside Larson's Pontiac, parked where overhead piping from the boiler area crossed the road and began to spread throughout the plant. Here it partly muffled the ripping high-pressure steam blasting from the top of No. 3 boiler. He slid out of the pickup, taking a good look around, and quickly stepped over to the concrete floor surrounding a multitude of battleship-gray pumps, where a white maze of pipe ran in all directions.

Everything outdoors was weatherproofed except the banks of recording and control instruments. The draft gauges were housed in a sturdy fireproof building, which was centered under the towering boilers. A tarpaulin was hanging over No. 3 boiler feed pump, and Barney headed that way. Two men in soiled gray coveralls were crouched over the governor end of the large turbine-driven pump and both straightened up as he rounded their shelter.

Sandy-haired Ed Burke, the ruddy-faced helper, broke into a quick smile. Adam Smith, the thin, gray-headed machinist in charge, pushed a soiled cap from his troubled forehead at seeing Barney. Slowly Adam shook his head and drug out a blue bandanna, beginning to polish the shatterproof lenses of his spectacles.

"Hi, fellows," Barney cried above the racket. "Where's Larson?" He leaned over to have a look at their work.

"Scott went to look for parts, Mr. Ranger." Adam Smith mopped his face, then replaced the spectacles.

"Parts?" Barney stared at the elderly machinist. "You don't need parts to adjust the over-speed trip."

Adam Smith looked down his long nose. "It ain't the over-speed trip, Mr. Ranger. It's that complicated latch in the throttle mechanism, the Z-shaped gadget that holds the over-speed safety. It won't hold no more."

"The hell it won't!" Jesus, this really was trouble.

Ed Burke shook his head solemnly. "No, Sir. Before she gets up speed she runs through a harmonic. That damn latch shakes off. Acts exactly like the over-speed had tripped," he said sharply. "We can't get her up to her normal thirty-six hundred revolutions." Ed gazed into Barney's face thoughtfully: "You know, I never seen a harmonic at thirty-three hundred before...." His voice trailed off.

"We tried to hold that latch in place, Mr. Ranger." Adam shook his head. "Tried to hold the rascal while the machine ran through that rough spot. But we couldn't do it."

"No, Adam, I wouldn't think you could." He leaned over for a closer look, still hoping that he might be wrong.

"This here's all right." Adam worked the overspeed trip against its coiled spring. "It'll work. But that darn latch won't hold no more. She's buggered, Mr. Ranger. Buggered."

Barney straightened up. "How do you mean, buggered?" He studied Adam's thin face closely.

"I mean she's worn out." Again the old machinist shook his head. "Just worn out till she shakes off. And I don't think Scott Larson will find another one."

"Hell, we've got to find one, Adam," he said sharply. "Or make one. This damn pump positively has got to run tonight."

"She'd be mighty tough to make," the old man drawled. "I don't think we can do it." Adam looked sideways at his helper.

"Here comes Scott now," Burke cried, pointing toward the boiler control room.

Barney watched Larson dodge through the whining machinery, moving toward them in a slow trot, his compact body was wrapped in flopping coveralls.

"Hi, Barney," Scott yelped, diving in under the tarpaulin. "Here's the gadget that's causing all the grief." He held out a small steel casting in the shape of a Z, with a pivot hole reamed just off center in the diagonal.

Taking the defective latch he held it up to the light. He could see nothing wrong, not until Larson's oily finger pointed to one tip. "You've got to catch it just right, Barney. See where the damn thing's worn."

"Oh, yes," he said, slowly turning the two-pound casting back and forth, scowling.

"It sure don't take a hell of a lot," Scott Larson agreed. "But it's enough. That bastard shakes off at thirty-three hundred, every damn time." He frowned shaking his mat of short brown hair, all the time watching Barney examine the worn tip of the casting. "How about putting her back together and forget the governor?" Scott asked cautiously. "We could run her on hand throttle."

"Oh hell no!" Barney was astounded. "That way you'd have no overspeed trip at all." He recalled once having seen a trip fail and the runaway machine had exploded from pure centrifugal force. "Scott, the damn wheel's already out of balance. It's running rough and it wouldn't have to get much out of control to wreck itself. The goddamn thing would rip out jagged chunks of steel like shrapnel." He lowered the defective casting, trying to keep from glowering at Larson: "I guess you don't have this piece in stock."

"No, Sir," Scott said quickly.

"Tonight you've got to put No. 3 in the header, Larson. What the hell are you going to do?" He searched the power foreman's face, then, lifting hard blue eyes, glared at the plume of steam ripping off the top of the No. 3 boiler.

"She's practically up to pressure now, Barney." Larson's troubled face had turned with his. "If we just had this goddamn feed pump."

"Look," he growled, putting his head close to Larson's face. "You fired this boiler too goddamn fast. Just look up there at that blast of steam."

"Everything was going all right, Barney," Scott said. "Until we had to tear into this damn pump governor. Then she got away from me."

"What the hell have you got operators for?"

Scott winced. "I guess they weren't on the ball," he said, avoiding Barney's stare.

"No, I guess not."

Adam Smith and his sandy-haired helper were waiting quietly for orders. Barney turned back to the dismantled governor. Scowling, he took the worn casting. There had to be a way out.

"Scott!" he yelped, tired of the deafening blast of steam.

"Yes, Sir?" Larson whirled.

"Why in the name of God don't you slow down the fire under No. 3 and put a stop to that goddamn racket?"

Then, barely cracking a smile, "There's not one process operator in the whole damn plant who can sleep with all that noise." He nodded at the defective governor. "It's going to take a while to fix that damn thing before you can run your feed-water pump."

Scott took two steps. "I'll stop the noise." Then he turned half around. "How you going to fix it, Barney? Make a new piece? Or build up that worn spot and machine it off?"

"Neither, I hope." He smiled grimly. "Either way would take far too long. We'd have to trim and file and fit and fool around for hours."

Scott looked nonplused. "Just what the hell are we going to do then?"

"First thing is to get the rag out and stop that goddamn atmospheric bleed," he said sharply. Then, motioning toward the machinist and helper, "Keep these men here, Scott. I'm going over to have a look at the records. I think they'll show that we've got a duplicate of this damn machine down in the feed prep section. And if there is, maybe we can steal the piece off of it." He grinned hopefully.

"By God!" Larson's face lighted up. "I sure do hope so." He whirled to the mechanics. "You guys wait right here. We'll soon have work to do," he grinned wheeling around and trotting off toward the boilers.

Barney stepped over to the two men, both staring with wonder at Larson's sudden exuberance. "Why don't you go ahead and put the governor back together, Adam? Except for this damn latch." He held up the worn casting. "There's a chance we can rob one from that big turbine in the feed prep area." He smiled reassuringly.

"Go as far as you can, Adam. And if you get through before I get back, take Ed and go down and have a look at the feed prep charge pump."

"Okay, Mr. Ranger," Adam said. "Darned if I don't think you've got something there." Adam's eyes sparkled and motioned to his young helper, "Come on, son. Let's get busy."

Carrying the light casting, Barney strode off down the aisle between whining pumps, taking a short cut to the plant office. He fished out his keys, juggling the casting in one hand while unlocking the door to his office.

He flipped on the lights, glanced at the tier of blueprints temporarily stuck on the green wall, and from the bookcase lifted a massive leather-bound volume. Moving around a couple of red upholstered chairs to his desk, he rapidly thumbed through pages that were an index of every single rotating machine in the Roanoke Plant.

In five minutes he verified the turbine drive on the feed prep charge pump. It was identical in every way with that broken-down machine at the boilers. Shoving the book aside he began thinking of what yet must be done. Changes that only he or Roger Slocum could authorize.

Suddenly he wished he'd delegated more responsibility to Jerome Jenks during the past three years when he was breaking in young Jenks as his assistant. As plant engineer, Jerome had the job of coordinating and timing maintenance to plant operation. He had been required to learn much about processing, had worked hard at the job, and deserved to be rewarded with more of the responsibility. But whenever Barney proposed giving young Jenks more authority, Roger Slocum always flatly refused, saying that Jenks already had a full-time job. That Jenks was far too young and inexperienced to be trusted with any part of the plant operation. Slocum seemed to have forgotten how young he himself had been at the starting up of Roanoke's Albany plant. Barney even half-suspected Slocum of deliberately holding Jerome back.

If so, it was a big mistake, for Jenks was closely related to Col. Gregory Lee Watson, the Louisville millionaire who owned Roanoke Chemicals and had founded the Watson Oil Company. Surely the colonel must have an especial goal in mind for this young man, and he couldn't possibly understand Slocum's attitude. He's always liked Jerome, tall, blond and very personable, who had been a regular guest all last summer at his and Hazel's patio cookouts, often a threesome. One particular evening Hazel had inquired how millionaires got their start.

Jerome, who had brought the sirloins and was acting as chef, had laughed: "I can tell you how Cousin Gregory got his."

With the steaks broiling and sizzling over charcoal, he told them how breeding thoroughbreds on Colonel Watson's bluegrass farm had been too tame, and how as a young man, with his annual auction of yearlings, the colonel had taken a flyer and had drilled for oil on land he had leased in the Rowan County hills.

This had turned out to be a very deep well. When the drilling crew knocked off for Christmas, the colonel (who was convinced he had nothing but a dry hole) had slipped out alone to the location on Christmas night and "salted" his well. He poured the hole nearly full of crude oil from the fuel tank, and the next morning when the crew began to clean out the hole, the first bailer had come up loaded with bright green crude indicating oil. This news quickly hit the Cincinnati papers and before the year had ended, the colonel sold to the Syndicate which controlled Newport and Covington.

With this money he founded the Watson Oil Company (of Texas). Later he purchased Roanoke Chemicals, Inc. Both corporations had been consolidated into the Amelia Watson Trust, Jerome explained, his blue eyes lighting up as the sirloins came off the grill, "Cousin Amelia is the colonel's wife."

Barney picked up the casting, thinking that Jerome never leaned on the colonel for power or influence. Neither did he slight his own work. He turned off the lights, thinking how pleased he had been with Jerome ever since he came on the job. Locking his office, Barney hurried toward the control house in search of Ralph Pettit.

The laboratory sampler, on a motor-scooter, bore down the street toward him. Barney waved him on as the shattering noise from the boiler vent suddenly ceased.

In the sudden quiet, his trained ears began to pick up the drone of machinery, selecting the peculiar whine of the hydrogen compressors, the chattering of an over-sized control valve in the solvent unit, the chuckling exhaust of the gas engine driving the plant air compressor.

Few visitors were allowed near the control house, which had been designed to withstand fire and explosion. It was a fortress-like building especially contrived to house the innumerable electronic devices that governed the operation of the entire plant. Those who were allowed to see this were always amazed. Colonel Watson always made the control house the first stop of his annual tour of inspection.

He'd always liked the affable colonel. Liked his boyish enthusiasm for electronic devices. Liked the way he wore a broad-brimmed Panama cocked on his silvery head, and the way he always seemed to be fascinated by the graphic control board. He had encouraged Girdler Corporation design engineers to gold plate the control system with an intricate system of interlocks, the first of its kind. And eight years of operation had thoroughly convinced Barney that without these interlocks, Director Paul Brossard's complex method of hydrocracking would be impossible to operate. "Automation truly was a very lovely thing," the colonel always declared, his shrewd blue eyes watching delicate adjustments made to achieve a maximum yield of their aromatic chemical product.

Barney stepped inside (air pressure constantly maintained within the building aiding him to pull open the heavily insulated door) and noted slender, high-strung Shift Foreman Pettit in the center of the room studying the master printer that was built into a desk-like console. The door swung to as Barney paused, waiting for his eyes to adjust to the light from a double row of fixtures in the soft white ceiling. All outdoor sounds were now shut off. It was as if he had walked into a huge and highly illuminated vacuum bottle.

Sensing a variation in the air pressure, Ralph Pettit swung around in his chair. He wore slacks and a sport shirt, a square-billed cap shading the keen eyes in his mobile face. Smiling briefly he at once swung back to the forest-green console.

Barney crossed the green terrazzo floor and laid the casting on the desk. He stood beside the shift foreman and carefully scrutinized the pale green instrument panel. Eighty feet long it rose from floor to ceiling on three sides of the room, a mammoth engineering flow diagram of the entire chemical plant. On the panel every major piece of equipment was symbolized in color: furnaces, towers, vessels, valves, both hand-operated and automatic, all included in the network of interconnecting pipe and tubing.

Everywhere colored lights flashed on and off. Barney was glad to see none of the flashing lights were red.

Under Plexiglas on the console, a three-foot-wide master chart crept endlessly from one roller to another. He leaned over with Pettit to examine the data coming up. His eyes followed the electronic scanner frantically printing a summary of the prevailing operating conditions. "What are you so intent in watching, Ralph?"

"Tower No. 6 in the superfractionator, Barney. The top temperature's been wobbling as if there was flooding down in the column." Pettit's finger picked out one line of numbers from the many on the chart (temperatures, pressures, flow rates) constantly received from the plant by instruments set into the wall-panel flow-diagram. "It looks stable enough now," he commented.

"What did you do to straighten it out?" Barney noted some hasty fluctuations recorded on the chart about twenty minutes back.

"Dropped the base temperature five degrees, Barney," Pettit said, pointing. "Then eased it back up three. After she cleared up."

"That was the right thing to do." He patted Pettit's shoulder lightly. "It's a cardinal law of physics that a vapor-liquid mixture can't be squeezed, without overloading the tower."

"Yes, Sir." Ralph tipped back in his swivel chair. "That's benzol stock and it's got to be steady." He picked up the worn casting. "What's this, Barney?" he asked, looking it over.

"Part of a pump governor. It's off the turbine driving No. 3 boiler feed-pump. See, this tip's worn away."

"Is this why that damn boiler's been blowing its top?" Pettit leaned on the console, again gazing at the creeping chart.

"You're damn right," Barney said sharply. "And it's got to be fixed, Ralph. We've got to have all three boilers on the line before you can start shutting down tomorrow."

"The hell you say!" Pettit straightened up. He looked at the casting, then at Barney. "Anything we can do to help out?"

"You sure can. The turbine on your feed prep charge is a duplicate of the one on No. 3 boiler. We've got to cannibalize this piece off of it."

"Hell, you can't do that, Barney." Pettit shoved his chair back and got up scowling. "We've got the big charge pump running."

"There's two charge pumps on the feed prep," Barney said quickly, then sensing a sudden change in the sound level of the room he turned toward the door.

Slim Goble came in, and with him the outside drone of machinery until the door closed. Goble was as tall as Barney, with light hair, and wearing khaki trousers. He shucked his leather gloves and, unzipping a suede jacket, moved across the green terrazzo.

"Hi, Barney," the feed prep stillman grinned, brown eyes twinkling. "You got your days and nights mixed up? We don't shut down till tomorrow." He pitched his gloves on the console. "No. 6 looks okay now, Ralph. She made a hell of a lot of bottoms for a while after we lowered the reboiler temperature. But she settled down, and the overhead product was always good." He bent over to look at the console chart.

"Okay, Slim, that's fine." Pettit nodded briefly. "And Barney's not got his days mixed up. He's got a problem."

"Who hasn't?" Goble's clear eyes questioned Barney. "What seems to be the trouble?"

"Scott Larson needs a casting like this," Pettit said quickly, pointing to the Z-shaped piece Barney held in his hand. "He said Larson's got to have it before he can make enough steam for us to shut down. So he wants to steal it off our big feed prep pump."

"Hell's fire, Barney, Larson can't do that! That pump's on stream."

"It's my idea, fellows," he said quickly, sensing the undercurrent of animosity ever-present between operators of processing units and those who supplied utilities. "It's not Scott Larson's," Barney said firmly. "We've got to have that boiler on tonight. And we've got to have the feed-water pump first." He held up the defective casting. "Except for the one you have, that one on your big turbine, I don't suppose there's another closer than the factory in New Jersey." He looked pointedly from one to the other. "So we are going to rob your pump."

Pettit shrugged and Goble shifted his feet thoughtfully.

"Put on your small charge pump." He tried not to sound impatient. "And slow down the unit if you have to. We're going to shut down the whole thing tomorrow anyway."

"Jesus Christ, Barney," Pettit moaned. "That means we've got to change flow rates all the way through. Don't it, Slim?"

"How come Larson ain't got parts for his stuff?" Goble demanded.

"What matters now is that we've got to put that boiler in the goddamn header." Ignoring Goble, he looked quietly and determinedly at the shift foreman. "You fellows are too damn allergic to change. Months of steady running and you stiffen up. Operators are about as

86

mechanized as the goddamn plant. Automation!" Barney shook the casting, glaring at the two men. "Maybe this plant runs too goddamn steady." Quickly he strode away, feeling both men watching silently. Then after a second, he turned and walked back to the console. "What's the level in those tanks between the feed prep and the hydro? Seems to me they were pretty well filled this afternoon."

Pettit dug a pad of tank gauges from the drawer, laid it on the console and ran his finger down a column of figures. "One is full, Barney. The other gauged twelve-foot-two at 4:00 P.M."

"Over a tank and a half," he nodded, verifying the gauges with a glance.

"There's fifteen hundred barrels of surplus stock you can use. That added to production will let you hold a steady charge to the hydro until we begin to shut down. You only have to change one section of the plant."

The stillman nodded glumly. It was his job to change pumps and stay on top of the operation until everything was adjusted.

"Now, Ralph," he said turning to Pettit, "let's get the show on the road. You have Slim switch those pumps, and switch them fast, so we can cannibalize the big machine."

"Take your No. 1 helper, Slim, and switch the goddamn feed prep charge pumps in a hurry." Pettit said. "And telephone me every time you make a change. I'll keep an eye on everything in here."

"Okay." Goble zipped up his suede jacket and reached for his gloves. "The first damn thing will be to reduce the charge rate," he mumbled, shooting a glance at Barney and tramping out of the building.

"Make him hurry it up, Ralph," he urged as the door closed. We haven't got all night."

"Sure thing, Barney," Pettit nodded. "I'll push it right along."

Starting toward the door, and anxious to get back to see how the work on the governor assembly was progressing, he heard Pettit call and whirled around.

"Don't you think I'd better call Jake?" Pettit fingered the bill of his cap.

Barney hesitated. Jake Warwick was highly sensitive about his position as foreman, and if Warwick was irritated, he raised hell with his men.

"Okay. Tell him that I'm on the job, and don't let anything slow down that pump switch. If there's any question, refer Jake to me."

Pettit nodded and picked up the telephone, and Barney suddenly remembered that he had to call Hazel. He glanced at the clock high on the instrument panel. Jesus Christ! He'd promised to call three-quarters of an hour ago.

Seeing Pettit lean on the console, Barney realized that he had better call Hazel from another phone and hurried out of the control house.

At the corner of the solvent unit he met Adam Smith and Ed Burke. "You got that governor together, Adam?" Barney asked, looking beyond Adam toward the shrill sound of a warning whistle from the boiler area.

"Far as we can go without that Z-shaped gadget," the machinist said. He turned and looked back over his shoulder as the whistle stopped. Burke dropped the heavy tool kit from his shoulder to the ground. "Watch them tools, Ed," Adam said, scowling.

"We're on the way to the feed prep now, Barney."

"Go ahead and have a look at that big turbine. It's a duplicate of the one you've been working on. Here's your pattern, Adam." He handed over the casting.

"Be damn sure to stay in the clear. The operators are going to have their hands full for a while. And don't you make a move till I get there," he said with emphasis.

Adam nodded. "We'll just look her over and get everything ready." Burke grunted, shouldering the kit.

Barney hurried on to an outdoor telephone mounted in a sound-proof cubicle. He pulled out the handset and dialed downtown, then his house number.

Waiting for Hazel to answer he leaned on the box, staring through the aisle toward No. 3 feed pump and wondering if that shrill whistle had been a low water level warning as Hazel came on the line. There followed a half-heard conversation, interrupted by more whistles and alarms, with him promising to leave the plant very soon.

An hour later he was ready. The feed prep was coasting along at reduced charge. And at last he was satisfied with the performance of the troublesome feed-water pump. He was pleased that there was still time to secure the boiler and protect tomorrow's shut down, that Scott Larson would be able to put No. 3 on the line.

The main gate closed behind him, and he leaned forward over the wheel to glance up through the top of the windshield. A few stars were peering through the broken clouds racing overhead. He was glad the threat of rain had lessened. It would be a good night at the country club.

His headlight beams swung away from the multi-windowed main office, sweeping across the well-kept lawn as he rounded the circle into Roanoke Avenue. He sighed gratefully, his complicated schedule for the next two weeks was set up. Lighting a cigarette, he kicked the brakes and stared out across the grassy strip of park land for a last look at the boilers.

Scott Larson had plenty of water-pump capacity now and No. 3 boiler was fired up again. All three of the stubby, out-sized venturi stacks now belched out equal amounts of flue gas to be swept away by the wind into a second stream of blue haze from the hydro chimneys. He listened to the whine of pumps and compressors and ran his eyes over a cluster of towers floodlighted against the dark sky.

High overhead twin flares flickered in the sky. Tomorrow there would be a hell of a lot of gas to get rid of, and both of those flares would wave long, orange plumes of roaring flame.

He eased the pickup away from the curb. To the north and beyond Albany's squared-off streetlights by the Lakeview addition, he tried to pick his home, seeing the beams of a car move along one street then swing toward the French Lick road. That might have been Hazel leaving the house. He was able to make out the country club farther out on the rim of Lake Breckinridge. There would be a good crowd for the party tonight, he thought, stepping on the gas.

When a woman reads a novel, a short story, a play, or any piece of fiction that is written by a female author, she is not surprised to learn about the type of shade on the living room lamp, the style of the furniture that is most prevalent, and the fashions of the moment. All of these things are expected and accepted so long as they advance the plot and are not just thrown in with no relevance.

When a woman reads the same type of writing by a male author,

she doesn't expect these things even if she would find them to be rel-
evant. Few men include this information because they seldom pay at-
tention to it. Harry Handy was the exception to this rule.

   In Chapter 5 of his novel, he gives full reign to his ability to estab-
lish a setting. He gives his reader more information about Lucy Jenks,
her life, her home, her friends, than he could have in any other way.
We find this to be so exceptional, that it must be mentioned.

—*Helen Howe*

5

   Just before seven o'clock Lucinda Watson Jenks cautiously opened
the door of her sitting and bedroom suite and tiptoed over the glossy
oak floor of the upstairs hall. It was Sunday and following the excitement of yesterday's Kentucky Derby she thought her five house guests
should sleep at least another hour.

   Pausing at the head of the stairs, she laid a slender competent hand
on the carved walnut newel post and listened. There was no sound from
behind the closed doors. Only the slow tick of the tall clock in the lower
hall broke the indoor silence. Outside in the warm early morning sun
catbirds, robins and cardinals exulted. Breathing deeply she sensed a trace
of aroma from the red rambling rose budding at the sill of the window.

   She was slender, of medium height with an erect carriage, had an
aquiline nose, candid deep blue eyes beneath dark brows and pale
golden wavy hair. Now shoulder length, though usually she wore it in
a swirled roll. This morning she was dressed in a soft yellow sweater
with short sleeves, full white skirt with a narrow gold belt, and white
moccasins with gold beading. Her delicately tanned skin glowed with
excellent health and though she would be forty-seven next month, in
the soft light of the hall she looked a good fifteen years younger.

   Ears still tuned for the sound of any movement, Lucinda turned
from the stairs and slipped quietly through the upstairs hall toward the
open double French doors and the front balcony. The hall was room-
sized, broad enough to be furnished with a pair of rosewood pedestal
tables, each bearing an antique hand-painted china lamp and flanked
by rose-carved chairs with needlepoint seats, a secretaire and an old
fashioned chest of drawers of tiger-striped maple wood. Oval hooked

rugs lay scattered over the polished oak floor while candelabra brackets hung at eye level on the cool gray walls. Watercolors she had painted years ago added just a touch of color.

Standing at the French doors she looked out over an iron-railed balcony sheltered by the pale blue ceiling of a two-story porch. Beyond tall, white, fluted columns and over the roofs of houses below the hill was a broad valley ending at the willow-banked Ohio River. Hearing a throbbing exhaust from a tow of barges bucking up the current, she gazed across the river to the dark soil of the Indiana bottom land. It was check-rowed with a bright green pattern of new corn. Idly she wondered if the barge tow was headed for Cousin Gregory's Tell City terminal.

The stately fifteen-room pink brick house stood on the highest rise in Henderson, Kentucky, surrounded by two square blocks of garden and bluegrass lawn. Unobstructed by the hundred-year-old trees, the view fell away to woodsy bottoms on the southwest; to the north and east lay Henderson. The mansion faced west where the Ohio flowed southerly into a long, slow bend down the valley.

In the lower hall the grandfather clock solemnly announced seven and Lucinda turned away from the balcony, wishing Ann Davis would slip away from Phil and come downstairs before the others. Ann had been her best friend at Newcomb College and her maid of honor when she married Gerald on her nineteenth birthday. She wanted to talk to her about Jim Allison.

Jim Allison, also forty-seven, five-feet-ten and darkly handsome with smooth black hair and flashing dark eyes. Nicely chiseled features, a trim mustache and a slight pout to his lower lip. Though Jim had a gift of intense concentration that came up with very quick, precise decisions, he seemed always on the move. He thoroughly enjoyed every opportunity of pitting his intensity against all comers.

He was addicted to betting the horses, and owned and operated the JA Ranch, an eighty-thousand-acre spread north of Los Angeles. Preferring to live in the rambling Spanish-colonial hacienda, though he still kept an eight-room penthouse in Beverly Hills. He had married once and was divorced only two years ago.

Lucinda had first met him in Pasadena, following a rather hectic two weeks in San Francisco. She had dropped down to spend November with Ann and Phil Davis and Jim, being Phil's business partner and very close friend, had turned up often as a delightfully entertaining dinner guest. Caught by her golden beauty, Jim had prevailed upon the Davises to bring Lucinda out for a week on the JA Ranch. They rode and swam and played records for hours, picnicking, singing and dancing. At the end of a delightful week they had strolled hand-in-hand from the patio pool, out to the mesa's edge which overlooked his fertile irrigated valley. Under the California moon he had proposed marriage.

Dear Jim she thought. He loved her and needed her, and she liked Jim and liked California, and he owned it for miles. Beyond the rich green valley, a deserty stock range rolled away to high mountains faint in moonlight beneath a star-studded sky. With all this waiting for her, why, Jim insisted, did she live alone in the over-crowded Middle West and put up with its miserable climate? Only with difficulty had she managed to put him off, begging for time to consider and since that November night six months ago he had plagued her with telephone calls and telegrams, as well as welcoming every opportunity to be with her.

She had to reach a decision. It was not an easy decision to make. Some of Jim's past was what she wanted to talk about with Ann Davis. She trailed one hand along the glossy banister, thinking of the fifteen years since Gerald had crashed his small plane into a clump of sycamores near the river. A widow at thirty-one. She had adjusted, overcoming the initial shock, and much later found she actually enjoyed her freedom, especially as her son Jerome became settled and happy. Soon probably he would be married. She liked Frederica Kruger, charming and clever, and a beauty.

Jerome had Gerald's sensitivity and graciousness and had grown into a remarkable resemblance of her own father, Timothy Watson. Tall with powerful shoulders and the yellow Watson hair and dark skin, and like her father, Jerome had acquired a great store of knowledge plus the ability to get things done. With Cousin Gregory to see that he got along in the world, Jerome left no problem.

She swept a strand of golden hair from her forehead. Jim Allison's proposal was complicated and anything but easy to solve. Naturally it meant abandoning almost everything she had. All her cherished possessions: this beautiful home where she had grown up, as well as the rich grain and tobacco farm called the Homestead that was her birthplace. It seemed both were almost a physical part of her, containing most of her memories, her way of life, as if a future obligation somehow seemed to clutch at her, and she had a great trust to keep the two lovely old places alive.

Not for herself, no. For her son? She did not hold entirely with heritage. Fighting a lump in her throat she doubted that Jerome himself knew what his desires would be in ten years.

Would it mean anything to him at all if these inheritances were disposed of and were gone? Was she making a decision for both of them really? Did Jerome unwittingly need her strength behind him, unspoken and unknown in an intangible way? It was silly, but she did have to think of children not yet born.

Momentarily her deep blue eyes touched and caressed every detail of the beautiful furnishings in the lower hall: a soft Persian rug sweeping from the stairs to fan-lighted double doors, the enormous mirror in a gold-leaf filigree frame above the carved rosewood love seat on which she noticed a crumpled tweed jacket. Frowning slightly and wondering how Jerome's coat happened to be there, she walked over and picked it up. Shaking out the wrinkles, she carried it to a closet under the stairs and carefully hung it away on a wooden hanger, her glance angling off through a side corridor from the main hall past the downstairs powder room and a bedroom and out to a vine-covered walk. The brick walk to the carriage house reminded her to have the station wagon dusted off early this morning.

Suddenly the contents of the labyrinthine basement popped into her head. There was the heating and cooling plant and the laundry. Besides these a meat locker and in the chilled sub-basement another ventilated room for fresh fruit and vegetables. Stored away in another room there were trunks and sealed boxes, accumulated over forty years of living, it had all been relegated to the cellar.

Strolling into the living room, where in the slanting sunlight she adjusted a pair of sculptured bookends, moved an ivory ash try and turned an armchair slightly before the fireplace. She gathered up yesterday's scattered newspapers, stacked them neatly on a gate-leg table, then moved back to the hearth and standing on tiptoe took the silver model of an automobile from the mantel, turning it so that light falling through glass doors caught the 1926 Duesenberg engraving. Jim would have liked it, she thought, replacing the gleaming model. With a handkerchief she carefully wiped away her fingerprints and turned with a glance at the patio outside as she crossed the carpet, moving through folding doors into the parlor.

Here the china figurines needed straightening, the lamp shades were slightly awry. She lifted a pair of ebony African heads and adjusted the table evenly, then moved into the hall and past the front doors to the library paneled in light walnut which her father had used as an office.

Still no sound upstairs, she walked into the dining room. The long oval table was newly laid with snowy linen, a centerpiece of fresh peach-colored tea roses, glassware and silver gleaming with polish, and eight blue china breakfast plates. With only six people in the house, Hattie must have laid places for Jerome and Frederica, too. Those two had no intention of driving down here for breakfast and likely not for lunch, either.

Putting the two extra settings in the pantry she quickly rearranged the table for six, bending over the fragrant centerpiece to move jams and jellies within easy reach, then backed up giving it a nod of approval. She moved toward the pantry, swinging by the liquor bar to push through a copper-bound door into the kitchen. Sunlight made mirrors of a battery of copper utensils above the six-burner gas range, giving light to the large sky-blue room, There was a gleaming vinyl floor with glossy knotty pine cabinets and shiny sinks, and light brown Hattie was turning out biscuit dough at the counter under the window.

Near fifty, Hattie Green was a perennial thirty-nine, tall, strong and clean-cut. The woman had been with Lucinda for almost twenty years. A cook without peer and an immaculate housekeeper and when necessary Hattie drew extra help from an unlimited supply of relatives. Away on a visit Lucinda always left her in charge, knowing that whatever came up would be well taken care of, and more than once upon returning home she had found out-of-town friends comfortably settled in with Hattie in charge, her own reputation for Kentucky hospitality preserved.

"Good morning, Hattie."

"Morning, Miss Lucy." A smile showing her even teeth. She waved a flour-covered hand toward the stove. "Fresh coffee."

Selecting a heavy mug Lucinda filled it half with coffee and half with hot milk, poured from a jug warm in a pan of hot water.

"You sure look good this morning." Hattie looked her up and down with approval. "Almost like a college girl." Dark eyes returned to her biscuit dough.

"Thanks. You don't look so bad yourself." She liked the red checked apron Hattie had on over her white crisp house dress and her low-heeled red shoes. "Isn't it a beautiful morning?" She took her coffee to the yellow table by the door to the screened porch and summer kitchen. "Melvin still around? A small fire would be nice in the living room. Just a few sticks of birch." She glanced out toward the carriage house where Hattie and her younger second husband had an apartment.

"Melvin's not so good this morning." Hattie's face clouded. "I could lay a little fire though. Soon's these biscuits are ready to bake."

Lucinda quickly shook her head. "No you stay with the breakfast. We don't need a fire, only for looks. What's wrong with Melvin?"

Melvin Green was thirty-five and a veteran of both World War II and Korea. As chauffeur and handyman he took care of the grounds and any heavy work around the house. He left as a grounds-keeper at Audubon Park with his marriage to Hattie, and Lucinda had been very glad to give him work.

"He's got a head this morning." Hattie slapped the dough and reached for the rolling pin. "Hung over a little."

"I imagine he's got lots of company, " Lucinda smiled: How many thousands of people had been at Churchill Downs yesterday?

"Should of stuck with beer, but he got foolish." Hattie began to cut out biscuits, dipping them lightly in the melted butter and arranging them carefully in the pan. Watching the two pans go into the refrigerator all ready to pop into the oven when the guests came down, Lucy enjoyed her hot coffee. It was still very quiet in the house. "Hattie, are you having Homestead ham this morning?"

"Sure am, Miss Lucy. Got it already sliced. I'll make red-eye gravy, and there's fried mush and them big country eggs. Nothing better for breakfast."

Hattie was right. No other ham tasted like those sugar-cured and smoked on her farm. The old formula was a Homestead secret, first developed by Great Grandfather Watson and further improved by Lucy's mother. They always butchered three times on the farm, waiting for a good cold snap. Hickory wood smoke finished up the hams in the spring, giving them that special, delectable flavor.

"I don't think anybody could have done better than that." She rose from the table and walked over to rinse her coffee mug, staring for a moment out through the open window. "Hattie, you have to be born a cook!"

EXTRACT FROM A MAY 19, 1964, LETTER TO JON SHIROTA FROM LOWNEY HANDY

I don't know about Harry's book. I've had it at some top places, and much enthusiasm has been shown. "Clever, good writing, fine and amusing characters, original," and they like the book muchly—but fear publishing a dead man.

—Courtesy of Jon Shirota

JON SHIROTA

Remembering Lowney Handy

By Jon Shirota

I first heard of Lowney Handy in the early fifties when James Jones' *From Here to Eternity* came out and Lowney was hailed as Jones' mentor and benefactor. Having been stationed in Schofield Barracks where most of *Eternity* takes place, I was, of course, enthralled, captivated, and deeply moved by the novel. I began envisioning the day I would meet Jones and Lowney and tell them of the pending great novel of mine. I even wrote Jones, telling him of my idea and that I was stationed in the same quadrangle as he was. He did not reply.

That, however, did not deter me. I was obsessed. I had to, and someday would meet the phantom lady, Lowney Handy. I just knew she would love my novel; she would immediately invite me to join her writers' colony.

When, at last, my novel was finished, I wrote Lowney Handy in Marshall, Illinois. I received a reply right away. She asked me to send her the first chapter of my novel. I mailed it that day. I was ready to quit my job and haul off to Southern Illinois at a moment's notice.

A response arrived from Lowney in a few days. Nervously, and with great anticipation, I tore open the envelope. I expected a glorious invitation. Instead, on the title page of my manuscript was inscribed a bold and unmistakable, "SHIT!" It did not end there. There were even more scathing and invective denunciations in the following pages. With tears clouding my eyes, I was made to realize that I did not know the first thing about writing.

There was, however, encouragements between her epithets. "If you are willing to learn to write," she said, "I can help you. I am not an agent or a publisher. I am a teacher."

And so began my long and arduous odyssey. I corresponded with Lowney from 1959 to 1963, sending her chapters of my reorganized and revitalized manuscript. She would return them with remarks and comments written all over the pages from top to bottom, side to side, backwards and frontwards. It was indeed a wild, painful, unpredictable, and at times, suicidal journey.

But learning I did! Dreaming of writing does not a writer make, she pounded in me. One goes to medical school to become a doctor; one must serve his apprenticeship to become a writer. She said it simply and viciously; she said it with love and unforgiveness. "I am cruel in order to be kind...."

Lowney Handy was a lady who knew no other way to express herself other than her own honest, brutal and loving way.

Extracts from an April 21, 1959, letter to Jon Shirota from Lowney Handy

1748 East Second St.
Tucson, April 21, 1959

Dear Jon:

Yesterday I marked your manuscript, rather severely, and returned it. Today, I began thinking that you might feel all the markings on the manuscript meant you were a bad writer. Which they did not mean at all. In fact I think I would have done better not to have put any marks on it—as many of the criticisms—or comments—were about life in general. Actually you write a smooth well constructed sentence, and I can see that you are groping toward a good style, and have much to say.

A beginner always looks bad, his stuff appears in a bad light, and 75 percent of the reason is he doesn't know technique. As Pope once wrote: "He moves easiest who has learned to dance," and this is true in writing. The ease of handling a scene—the know-how of writing one—or getting in and out—the transitions into a scene or a chapter sometimes are as important as the chapters or scenes themselves.

In fact I can recall when Jones—in Eternity—put as much time and thought and labor on the transitions as he did the entire chapter. If you want to see what I mean, look at the last page of a chapter and the beginning first page of the next. Not only in *Eternity* but in *Running* is this very pointedly so.

Now a writer when he begins to write, will do so out of a hurt, a

99

vast feeling of inferiority. You won't think this is so, but I have seen it again and again. It is the springboard. It is your own absorption with your own agony that moves you to explain it—and also the agony of others you have met. Maybe, a writer while starting out is not using common sense enough, and his sentimental or emotional reaction is such that he is involved almost sentimentally with another. This isn't bad. Walt Whitman said: "I do not pity the wounded person, I myself, become the wounded person." This is empathy, which is much stronger than sympathy. It means a complete association, and you have to be sensitive and also able to forget your own agony—in the understanding of another's which is to be able to take the second place. We are all so absorbed with our own agonies, that to give a brief second or two in which we forget our own individual personal self-centered self, to monetarily—BECOME THE WOUNDED PERSON of someone around us—shows that here you have a writer—because the masses cannot free themselves at all....

The first thing to learn is SELF-FORGETFULNESS—not to be self-centered—for self-centeredness means—hate, love, fear, anger, sorrow, self-love, self-hate, self-seeking, ambition, all the many things that are connected with you personally as an individual. A GOOD WRITER RISES ABOVE THESE THOUGHTS—

On the physical and emotional planes of existence—TIME AND PLACE ARE VERY MUCH A PART OF IT.

But when you learn to concentrate—you forget yourself and can be lost in work for half an hour—one hour—or ten minutes. It isn't known to you—you can forget your name, where you are and how long you have been there—THEN ON THE MENTAL PLANE TIME AND PLACE DO NOT EXIST. It is this rising above the everyday existence—above time and place—that you seek to learn concentration. Without it you cannot be a great writer. And anything that increases your ability to concentrate or to forget yourself is very very beneficial and promising for a future as a writer.

So in copying, you not only learn the know-how—the technical rules and best methods to write well, but you learn that terrifically important thing of being able to escape yourself. To rise above the present—and that way your higher mind—your oversoul—as Emerson wrote about—the superconscious self in you will unite with the subconscious self—and things will be given you to put on paper that will astound you.

Like the Phoenix bird you rise above the dead ashes of the past— and in so doing the doors of the future are opened—and a real genius of a writer is born. BUT NOT UNTIL THE WRITER CAN LEARN HOW TO ESCAPE HIS OWN LITTLE ORBIT OF HIS PERSON- ALITY OR INDIVIDUAL SELF-SEEKING SELF....

—*Courtesy of Jon Shirota*

In April of 1963, when Lowney said I was ready to come to her Colony to finish my novel, I quit my job as a U.S. Treasury agent and was on my way to Marshall, Illinois, the following day.

After a hectic two-day drive, I arrived at the Handy Writers' Colony and was greeted by a dilapidated sign on the gate: THE LAST RE- TREAT.

I discovered that the sign was put there by Jim [James Jones]. Lowney explained that it was Jim's way of saying that once you leave the Colony and go out into the world, you may return. But for the last time. For you know this is your LAST RETREAT.

I spent six lonely, isolated, but productive months at the Colony, and finally finished my first novel, Lucky Come Hawaii. *I had planned to return to the Colony, but Lowney suddenly died in 1964. And a part of me died with her.*

Years later, I would write a yet-to-be-produced play, The Last Re- treat, *in commemoration of my association with Lowney and the Handy Writers' Colony. Although the characters are fictitious, the protago- nist, Hilda Thatcher, is a composite of the Lowney Handy I knew, re- spected and loved dearly as I did my own mother.*

—*Jon Shirota*

THE LAST RETREAT

By Jon Shirota

INTRODUCTION

The Thatcher Writers' Colony is in Creighton, Illinois, a small rustic town two hundred miles south of Chicago. Situated on a sprawling ten-acre retreat of elms, maple and pine trees, it is isolated from the rest of the world.

There are several cabins spread over the secluded Colony, each furnished with only the bare necessities, a bed, a desk and a chair. In the heart of the Colony is the ramada, the cafeteria, where the residents have their meals and spend their leisure hours together. Beside it is a pear-shaped swimming pool, carefree squirrels, chipmunks and rabbits hopping about playfully. Beyond the pool is a row of pine barracks filled with reading materials.

Hilda Thatcher is the founder of the Colony, and the entire play takes place in the living room of her spare cabin. The room is devoid of modern conveniences, no TV, no radio, no phone. The shelves, however, abound with books, magazines and periodicals. It is an artistic room, not comfortable nor homey, but clean, orderly and purposeful. It is Hilda's sanctuary. It is where she reads, writes and meditates.

The main entrance is a squeaky screen door, Up Right. Just inside is a doorway to the kitchen. Up Center is a fireplace, firewood flanking it. The back entrance is another squeaky screen door, Up Left, beside it the door to the bedroom. Through a window between the fireplace and the back entrance can be seen parts of the mansion belonging to the Colony's first successful writer, Tom Wilson. The shelves on Left and Right are filled with books. The furniture, Center, consist of a pine bench, a couple of hard-backed chairs, a couch and a coffee table. Hilda's desk is Down Right.

CAST IN PLAY
(in order of appearance)

Hilda Thatcher	(white)
Alan Crenshaw	(white)
Tom Wilson	(white)
Eddie Hills	(black)

TIME
Spring - 1970

ACT ONE

Scene I	Living room of cabin. Noon.
Scene II	Same scene. An hour later.
Scene III	Same scene. That night.

ACT TWO

Scene I	Living room of cabin. Noon. Next day.
Scene II	Same scene. Four hours later.
Scene III	Same scene. That night. A few hours later.

ACT ONE, SCENE I

(Spring of 1970. Noon. We HEAR chirping and singing of birds. As lights gradually brighten, HILDA THATCHER, a gray-haired woman in early fifties, is banging away on an old typewriter, Down Right. Slim, trim, energetic, she is in Jeans and sports shirt, no makeup,

her expression a picture of utter concentration. After a moment, there is knock at front door, Up Right.)

HILDA

Come in!
(Continues typing)
(ALAN CRENSHAW, late twenties, exhausted from hours of writing, steps in. He is wearing faded Levis, rumpled shirt and a pair of unlaced GI boots. In his hand is a chapter of his novel.)
I'll be with you in a minute, Alan.
(Finally finishes typing. Taking out paper from typewriter, she places it almost ceremoniously on a heap of manuscript.)
I'm rewriting the last two chapters.

ALAN

Your novel?

HILDA

(Nodding)
I want you to read it; tell me what you think about it before I send it to the publisher.

ALAN

Sure.
(Looking through back window toward mansion)
He's back?

HILDA

Not yet.

ALAN

Maybe he changed his mind.

HILDA

He'll be here. If not today, tomorrow.
(Beat)
I don't think you should come here at nights while he's at the Colony.

ALAN
> That might be weeks. Months!

HILDA
> *(Shaking head)*
> Spencer Hoyt's got the papers ready to be signed, sealed and delivered on Monday.

ALAN
> What about your right of first refusal?

HILDA
> I can't match that old goat's offer. That slimy old geezer, he's been trying to run me out of town ever since we started the Colony. Looks like he's finally getting his wish.

ALAN
> You put this town on the map.

HILDA
> For drifters and bums according to that nincompoop.

ALAN
> *(Beat)*
> We still gonna be able to drive through the front gate?

HILDA
> Not with Hoyt owning that half of the property.

ALAN
> Talk to Tom. Make him change his mind.

HILDA
> In the old days, yes. Today...
> *(Shrugs)*
> I don't want you hanging around him.

ALAN
> *(Beat)*
> I always wondered if he actually knew the characters in *Above and Beyond*. What a bunch of great characters.

HILDA
> What's he written since? Not a damn thing.

ALAN
> I thought *Turbulence* was pretty good.

HILDA
> It stunk! Every bit of it!

ALAN
> What about...?
> *(Thinks better of it. Beat; pleadingly)*
> Hilda. Let me move back in.

HILDA
> No! Not as long as someone else is here.

ALAN
> Christ. First, it was Eddie returning. Now him.

HILDA
> Eddie knows?

ALAN
> So what if he knows?

HILDA
> *(Reaching)*
> Dear ... Please try to understand. There have been many other writers here before you. If word got out that I've been sleeping with you, my God! they're going to say I've slept with all of you writers.

ALAN
(Embracing)
Who cares what anyone says?

HILDA
(Holding him tenderly, maternally)
Begging, stealing and lying for the sake of writing is not enough,
Dear. You must harness your emotions, too. Direct every ounce of
it to your writing. Utterly.

ALAN
Is that all I mean to you? A writer?

HILDA
Of course not. I...have my needs, too. Even though I'm old enough
to be your mother.

ALAN
You promised! You're never going to bring that up again.

HILDA
Just reminding myself, Dear.

ALAN
What if Tom wants you to... You know...

HILDA
Stop that.

ALAN
He might expect you to...

HILDA
Stop it!
*(The pervading silence overwhelming. Finally, indicating manu-
script on floor)*
What's that?

ALAN
> *(Picking up manuscript; handing it)*
> Another chapter.

HILDA
> Another chapter? That's wonderful, Alan. At this rate you'll have
> your next novel finished in no time.

ALAN
> *(Beat)*
> Christ, it's over a month since we sent the first one out.

HILDA
> You just keep working on your next one.

ALAN
> How long did it take to sell Tom's first novel?

HILDA
> The publisher gave Tom an advance even before it was finished.
> The Second World War was just over. Publishers were looking for
> that great novel that comes out of every war.

ALAN
> The agent, you think he's having a tough time selling mine, the
> Vietnam War still going on?

HILDA
> If there's anyone who can sell it, it's Oliver Rasmussen.

ALAN
> What if the war doesn't turn out the way I'm saying it will?

HILDA
> Your novel will still be great.
> *(Reaching for chapter on desk; handing it)*

This chapter is good. But not nearly as good as you're capable of writing it.

ALAN

Mai isn't coming through?

HILDA

She comes through honestly for the most part. Now and then, you, the author, intrude and come in the way. I know it's not easy for you to write a woman. Tom had the same trouble. He just couldn't get it through his thick skull that women can be sweet and lovely and a horse's ass all at the same time. And for God's sake, Alan! Don't be moralistic. Leave the preaching to the preachers.

ALAN

Mai don't give a shit about morals.

HILDA

Then write her like that. In your first novel you became the GI characters. Now, in this novel, you must become Mai, the Vietnamese whore. Utterly. When she's making her rounds through the bull ring, you're her. When she's hurting going through a company of GIs, you're her. When she falls in love with the VC, you're her. Remember, "I do not pity the wounded; I become him." Also, "In all people I see myself. Not one barley corn less, not one barley corn more. The good and bad I say of them I say of myself."
(There is a loud persistent knock, Up Right.)
That goddamn Eddie! I swear I'm going to...!
(More knocking. Hilda grabs baseball bat and storms to door.)
You're going to get it this time!
(She stops in her track. Lowering bat, she stares through door. Sweetly)
Tom! Tom Wilson! My God! Is that you?

TOM (O.S.)

Not God, Hilda. Just me.

HILDA

Come in. For God's sake, come in.

TOM

(TOM WILSON steps in. In late forties, he is wearing a crumpled suit, wrinkled shirt, no tie. Slightly drunk, he stares at bat in Hilda's hand.)
Helluva way to greet someone you haven't seen over ten years.

HILDA

Has it been that long? Ten years? I can't believe it. Let me look at you. Why, you look no different from the day you left.

TOM

I look like I just jumped outta a pile of horse shit, and you know it.

HILDA

Now, that's not so.
(To Alan who is obviously awed by the presence of the famous writer.)
Isn't that right, Alan? Doesn't he look just wonderful?—Oh, I forgot. You two haven't met. Alan, this is Tom Wilson. The big-time Park Avenue writer.
(To Tom)
Alan is our next great West Coast writer.

ALAN

Hi, Tom.

TOM

(Shaking)
Hi, Kid. Our next great West Coast writer, eh?

HILDA

He's writing about Vietnam. The first one's already finished. He's now working on the sequel. They're going to be the greatest war novels of all times.

TOM

Hilda and her superlatives. The greatest or the shittiest.

HILDA

Alan spent over a year there. He was in the infantry. Like you were in the Pacific.

ALAN

I saw you in Nam.

TOM

Yeah. War correspondent for *Newsweek*. So you're writing about the Vietnam War.

HILDA

Oliver Rasmussen says it's the best thing he's read in years.

ALAN

I hope it'll be as good as *Above and Beyond*.

HILDA

Of course, it will.
(Pushing Alan toward door)
Now you go back to your cabin and work on that chapter we talked about. Then start working on the next chapter.

ALAN

(Leaving)
Nice meeting you, Tom.

TOM

Right, kid. See you around.
(Alan exits. To Hilda.)
Nice kid.

HILDA

He's going to be a great one. Has all the qualities, dedication, self-sacrifice, discipline.

TOM

Which I never had.

HILDA

Oh, I wouldn't say that. In the beginning, there was no one more sacrificing than you. —Where's Barbara? And your daughter?

TOM

They didn't come.

HILDA

You mean I don't get to meet that sweet wife of yours? Or your lovely daughter?

TOM

They're in Up-State New York visiting Barbara's folks.

HILDA

Up-State New York? —Oh, yes, of course. That must be in the upper part of New York state. Poor woman. Won't she miss all her Park Avenue friends?
(Beat)
So... When are you leaving?

TOM

I just got here.

HILDA

Where's your suitcase?

TOM

I left them at the mansion.

HILDA
Them?

TOM
(Beat)
I see my sign is still there on the gate.

HILDA
"The Last Retreat..." Everything in the mansion is the same as you left it. Your gun and knife collections, your boxing gear, your Army outfit, they're all still in the trunk.

TOM
(Stepping over to Hilda's desk, digs into coat pocket, brings out flask, and drinks. Indicating Hilda's manuscript)
Still working on your novel, I see.

HILDA
I'm doing the final rewrites.

TOM
Gotta hand it to you, Hilda. Eternal persistence; undying dedication.

HILDA
It gets better with every revision.

TOM
Like vintage wine, eh? So anyway... How's things going here in the Colony?

HILDA
Just fine. Several members had their novels published since you left. Nothing sensational. Achievements nevertheless. Alan's, of course, is going to be the...

TOM
—The greatest novel of all time...

HILDA
I'm not taking in anymore new writers.

TOM
How many you have now?

HILDA
Two.

TOM
Just two?

HILDA
A far cry from the old days when we had as many as twenty. But I was much younger then. Now, don't tell me you came back to expand the Colony.

TOM
Expand?

HILDA
I can't handle anymore new students, Tom. I'm past fifty.

TOM
Well, I was hoping we could... —Naw. You can't be fifty.

HILDA
I sure am.

TOM
But still as tough as nails.

HILDA
(No longer playful.)

All right. Let's cut out all this bull shit. What are you really here for?

TOM

See. As tough as ever.

HILDA

Yeah. And the bigger the ego the tougher I get.

TOM

I felt welcome for five minutes anyway.

HILDA

You don't tell me why you're back in five seconds you're gonna get your ass flying out that door!

TOM

Yep. Back in good old Creighton all right.

HILDA

(Beat)
I'm still waiting.

TOM

Goddamnit, Hilda! Can't a guy come back to his old hometown without a reason? In case you've forgotten, I still own a part of this place.

HILDA

Not that chair you're sitting on.

TOM

Ten years! And you treat me like I was gone ten minutes.

HILDA

Come back in another ten years. I might give you ten more minutes of my time.

TOM
(Takes another drink. Reciting)
"The trees grew taller, the grass turned greener. I got older and Hilda got meaner."

HILDA
(Steps over to desk, brings out key from drawer, and crosses to door, Up Left.)
Come on. You can do your drinking and passing out at your own place.

TOM
(Rising)
"Home, home, home at last
Ah, to be home at last
What does it get me?
A big kick in the ass"
(Lights gradually dim as he follows Hilda out.)

BLACKOUT

Act One, Scene II

(Same scene. An hour later. EDDIE HILLS is at bookshelf, Down Left, going through a book. A black in early thirties, Eddie is of medium height and wears scholarly glasses. He has on Levis, a work jacket over T-shirt and a pair of old leather sandals.

In a moment, Hilda enters, Up Left, slamming the door furiously. Not noticing Eddie, she crosses toward her desk, Down Right, muttering)

HILDA
...Playacting. Always playacting. Can't get anything out of him...

EDDIE
  Who, Mama?

HILDA
  (Startled, stops in her track. Sternly)
  Why aren't you in your cabin writing?!

EDDIE
  I just couldn't go on, Mama. —Who're you talking about?

HILDA
  (Ignoring, steps to desk.)
  Your typewriter broke down again?

EDDIE
  It's those birds on my roof. They keep arguing and chattering among themselves.

HILDA
  Tell them to go away.

EDDIE
  They won't listen to me.

HILDA
  Now, Eddie. Go back to your cabin and finish that chapter.

EDDIE
  I'm trying to, Mama.

HILDA
  Try a little harder.

EDDIE
  (Crossing, Down Right, toward Hilda, obviously wanting company)
  You almost done with your novel?

HILDA
> *(Going along patiently)*
> I'm doing the final rewrites.

EDDIE
> That's great, Mama. It's going to be a best-seller. I just know it will.

HILDA
> You almost done with your best-seller?

EDDIE
> Aw, Mama. You know I still have a long ways to go.

HILDA
> You do?

EDDIE
> It's only been a couple of months since I've been back. It sure seems longer.

HILDA
> Not if you've been keeping yourself busy.

EDDIE
> I have been keeping myself busy, you know that.

HILDA
> Writing?

EDDIE
> What else?

HILDA
> *(Looking all over her desk, playfully)*
> That's funny. I haven't come across any of your chapters lately.

EDDIE

I'll be handing you another one in a day or two.

HILDA

You will? I was beginning to think you're so busy counting the royalties from your first book you didn't have time to do any more writing.

EDDIE

Aw... I'm still not used to being back.

HILDA

Those naughty birds?

EDDIE

It's so damn quite in the cabin. Gives me the creeps.

HILDA

Even when you're banging away on your typewriter?

EDDIE

You can write just so much.

HILDA

You know the rules, Eddie. Four hours at the typewriter. Then, working in the yard and the garden.

EDDIE

I sure wish it's like it used to be. Hanging around the kitchen, shooting the bull and sometimes going into Terre Haute.

HILDA

Don't you and Alan get along?

EDDIE

That dude! If he's not busy writing, he's busy working on that car of his.
(Looking away, grinning)

I don't know where he goes at nights. He's never around.

HILDA

Maybe he has a girlfriend in town.

EDDIE

Yeah. That must be it.

HILDA

(Beat)
All right, Eddie. Visiting hours are over. Go back to your cabin and finish that chapter.

EDDIE

All right, Mama. I'll tell those naughty birds they better shut up or Mama Thatcher's be coming over with her BB gun.

HILDA

Yes, Eddie. You tell them that.

EDDIE

(After a few steps toward Up Right)
They might not listen to me, Mama.

HILDA

(Exploding)
Edward Hills! You get right back to your cabin and put in your four hours or I'm going to...!

EDDIE

But, Mama... Those birds...

HILDA

(Reaching for BB gun beside desk)
You mention those birds to me again, so help me! I'm gonna shoot your goddamn black ass so full of holes you're gonna wish you never left St. Louis!

EDDIE

(*Crossing to door, Up Right*)
I hear you, Mama. I hear you.
(*Door, Up Left, opens and Tom Wilson enters, a knife sheath attached to his belt.*)

TOM

Hey, Eddie!

EDDIE

Tom! Tom Wilson!
(*Rushes over, embraces*)
You no-good mother! Whendahell you get back?

TOM

Get back? I never left.

EDDIE

(*To Hilda*)
Shame on you, Mama. You never told me Tom was coming back.

TOM

(*Also to Hilda*)
And you didn't tell me Eddie was the other writer here.
(*To Eddie*)
Hey, man, how long has it been? Five, six years?

EDDIE

At least. Last time I saw you was at your agent's party on Lexington.

TOM

That long ago?

HILDA

All right, Eddie. You said your "hello". Get going.

EDDIE
Mama! This is Tom Wilson. My buddy.

HILDA
(Lifting rifle)
Edward Hills!

TOM
For Chrissake, Hilda! Eddie and I go back a long way.

EDDIE
Long, long way...

TOM
Hell, yeah. The good old days.

EDDIE
Oh, were they ever! Screaming, bubbling, ass-kicking days.
(Hilda pumps gun)
All right, Mama. All right. I'm already gone.
(Heads for door, Up Right.)
Catch you later, Tom.

TOM
Right, Eddie.
(Eddie exits. To Hilda)
Whattahell was all that about! That's Eddie.

HILDA
Who hasn't put in his four hours today.

TOM
Why don't you let up once in a while for Chrissake.

HILDA
What's the matter? Feeling guilty for not doing any writing?

TOM

Is that why you keep working on that novel of yours? To keep from feeling guilty?

HILDA

When my novel comes out you and all your New York cronies are going to know what good writing is all about.

TOM

And I'll be the first to congratulate you.

HILDA

Hogwash!

TOM

(Beat)
Hilda-Matilda, our nail-eating, ass-kicking, rifle-totting devotee of letters.
(Reciting)
"She spits, she bites, she farts
All in the name of the arts."

HILDA

That's lots more than I can say for you, Tom Wilson.

TOM

You can call me Tom. You can call me Harry. You can even call me asshole. Just don't let my mama catch you calling me that.

HILDA

(Beat)
I thought you were going through your knife and gun collections.

TOM

(Sips from flask.)
The walls, they kept closing in on me.

HILDA

Keep drinking you're gonna have snakes and buzzards closing in on you.

TOM

(Imitating)
"Hogwash!"

HILDA

You do whatever you want to do; just do it at your own place. And don't you ever let me catch you bothering Eddie. It took him weeks to get started, and you're not going to set him back!

TOM

You know me better than that.

HILDA

(Looks at him.)
Eddie's got more talent than you and all you New York cronies put together. His problem is discipline.

TOM

His problem is you. You've got him so scared of everyone out there he keeps running back to you. "Mama, Mama."

HILDA

He knows better than to hang around your Lexington Avenue friends.
(Suddenly looks at wristwatch)
Oh, Jesus! I have to be in Singleton in half an hour.
(Heading for door, Up Right)
Remember what I told you. Keep away from Eddie. And Alan, too.
(Exits)

TOM

(Muttering)
...She spits, she bites, she farts.
All in the name of the arts...

(Takes another drink, then restless, steps over to Hilda's desk and browses through her novel. Crossing to couch, he whips out knife and rubs it fondly, nostalgically. In a moment, Eddie returns.)

EDDIE
(Looking around)
Did she say where she was going?

TOM
(Placing knife back into sheath)
Down to Singleton.

EDDIE
(Relieved, crosses to couch)
That means she won't be back until tonight. Her sister's husband died last week.

TOM
Harry? Harry Campbell died?

EDDIE
(Nodding)
Hilda's been going down to help settle the estate.

TOM
What did Harry die of?

EDDIE
(Shrugging)
Heart attack, cancer or...something.

TOM
(Beat)
Harry Campbell dead... My high school classmate.
(Takes drink)
Won't be long before we'll all be gone. —Hey, man! How's everything been with you?

EDDIE
> Bitching. —It's good to see you, man. How long you staying?

TOM
> *(Suspiciously)*
> Hilda put you up to it?

EDDIE
> Up to what?

TOM
> Find out why I'm back.

EDDIE
> Hey, Tom, baby. This is Eddie. Your buddy.
> *(Beat)*
> I heard about you and your wife.

TOM
> You did, eh?

EDDIE
> You're back to write another novel?

TOM
> *(Nodding)*
> I...don't know if I can finish it.

EDDIE
> Why not?

TOM
> *(Stepping away, avoiding Eddie's eyes)*
> Time. Time's closing in on me. If I'm lucky, I'll finish it up there.
> *(Eddie looks at ceiling.)*
> I'm...dying, Eddie.

EDDIE
    Dying!

TOM
    I don't want anyone else to know. Okay?

EDDIE
    Tom! You're pulling my leg!

TOM
    (Beat)
    We all return from whence we came.

EDDIE
    Oh, man!

TOM
    Hey, buddy. It's not all that bad. I still have a few weeks.

EDDIE
    Weeks! Oh, God!

TOM
    (Beat)
    Too much of everything, the doctor said. Excesses, he called it.

EDDIE
    Smoking?
    (Tom nods)
    Drinking?

TOM
    (Nodding)
    And too much screwing. Whattahell... I've been living on bor-
    rowed times, anyway.
    (Raising flask flourishingly)
    Here's to you, Buddy.

EDDIE
(Tearfully)
Oh, God, Tom... Wasn't for you I would've never been a writer.
Why can't it be some motherfucker nobody gives a shit about!

TOM
Hey... Hey, Buddy. C'mon. I wouldn't have told you if I knew
you'd take it so hard.

EDDIE
You and Hilda, you're the only ones I have left in this whole
goddamn stinking world!

TOM
Oh, Christ, Eddie.

EDDIE
(Fighting back sobs)
Anything I can do for you? Anything!

TOM
Yeah, there is something you can do for me.

EDDIE
Name it, Tom. Just name it.

TOM
Just before they bury me I want you to open my casket.

EDDIE
Open your casket? What for?!

TOM
So I can stick my ass out and let go a loud fart.

EDDIE

(Stares at Tom who is suppressing laughter.)
You're not dying?

TOM

For Chrissake, Eddie.

EDDIE

(Rushing to Tom; hugging him)
You're not dying! Oh, thank God! You're not dying...

TOM

Hey... C'mon... Knock it off.

EDDIE

(Stepping back)
Tom Wilson! You no-good mother!

TOM

A scene from my next book, Eddie.

EDDIE

I should've known.

TOM

"...We all return from whence we came..."
(Chuckles)

EDDIE

You sonofabitch.
(Both laughing now)
I always said you missed your true calling.

TOM

I would've been one helluva actor.
(Takes sip)
Right now, I'm thinking of becoming a fisherman.

EDDIE
Fisherman?

TOM
A sports fisherman. In Florida. Buy myself a boat and be one with nature.

EDDIE
What about writing?

TOM
Fuck writing! I just want to be out in the ocean enjoying myself. Away from everything, from everyone.

EDDIE
You're not going back to New York? Hollywood?

TOM
Fuck New York! Fuck Hollywood!

EDDIE
I thought you liked it out there in California.

TOM
Bunch of assholes! —Hey, something wrong with Hilda?
(Eddie looks at him.)
She's not as tough as she used to be.

EDDIE
I wouldn't swear by it.

TOM
She never used to talk about kicking me out; she did it.

EDDIE
She was kind to me, too, when I first came back.

TOM
  That farm of hers, she still gets income from it?

EDDIE
  (Nodding)
  She also gets a little income from lecturing.

TOM
  The universities still invite her?

EDDIE
  They keep inviting her as long as she's running this Colony.

TOM
  (Looks at Eddie, deliberating)
  —Aw, she'll be all right. She'll always have that income from her farm.

EDDIE
  She always manages.

TOM
  They don't come any tougher. Remember the time she wanted to take on the whole police force in that hick town in Georgia?

EDDIE
  Do I? On our way to Florida.

TOM
  She knew goddamn well they wouldn't serve you in that restaurant. But there we were.

EDDIE
  All those rednecks ready to jump us.

TOM
  She sure was ahead of her time.

EDDIE
>Brother King could've taken a few lessons from her.
>*(Beat)*
>She ever tell you the first time I came here?
>*(Tom shakes head)*
>She was about to drop dead. "I'm Eddie Hills," I said. "Your blond, blue-eyed correspondent student."
>*(Tom laughs; Eddie joins.)*
>...Never said shit. Just pointed to the ramada kitchen. "Go get something to eat," she finally says.

TOM
>*(Beat)*
>Ever read that novel of hers?

EDDIE
>Huh-uh. Don't want to either. Don't ever want to criticize anything she writes.

TOM
>A helluva story about a young girl growing up in a mining town in Kentucky.

EDDIE
>Her?

TOM
>*(Nodding)*
>Been writing it for ten years now.

EDDIE
>And she's going to keep writing it the next ten years.

TOM
>*(Takes nip; offering)*
>Go on. Take a nip.

EDDIE

> Huh-uh. Sticking to Vermouth.

TOM

> Vermouth? Straight Vermouth?

EDDIE

> Gives me a glow without making me crazy. —Hey, man. I better get back to my cabin and finish that chapter I'm working on.

TOM

> You're going to leave me? When I'm dying?

EDDIE

> You go to hell, Tom Wilson.

TOM

> I'll see you there, Eddie Hills.

EDDIE

> *(Crossing, Up Right)*
> Taps. Remember to blow taps when I open your casket.
> *(Exits, laughing)*

TOM

> *(Chuckling, takes another sip. Pulls out knife from sheath and rubs it fondly. As he hums "Taps" nostalgically, lights begin to dim.)*

BLACKOUT

ACT ONE, SCENE III

(Same scene. That night. It is raining hard, lightning streaking past the window, thunder rumbling low in the dark skies. Tom is passed out on couch while Alan and Eddie are at fireplace, Up Center, warming themselves.)

ALAN
Christ! I thought the thunderstorms in the Northwest were bad.

EDDIE
You ain't seen nothing yet.

ALAN
(After another rumbling)
How can he (Tom) sleep through all this?

EDDIE
A whiff of booze and he'll be up and running.

ALAN
(Beat)
I hope my roof's holding up.

EDDIE
A herd of elephants gonna be pissing on it before the night's over.
(Alan looks at him.)
Never hails in the Northwest?

ALAN
Is a gorilla's ass red?

EDDIE
(Beat)
Have any grass on you?

ALAN
　What?

EDDIE
　Grassie, grassie, senor. Por favor.

ALAN
　No habla espanol.

EDDIE
　(Sings)
　La cucaracha, la cucaracha Marijuana que fumar...

ALAN
　(Digging into pocket)
　It just so happens...
　(Brings out joint)

EDDIE
　Oh, senor! Mucho mucho.

ALAN
　Poquito, poquito.
　(Sticks joint back into pocket.)

EDDIE
　You're a mean mother, you know that.

ALAN
　(Relenting, brings joint back out.)
　We better not do it here.

EDDIE
　He (Tom) won't mind.

ALAN
　Hilda.

EDDIE
> Mama? She don't know a joint from burnt cow turd. C'mon, man.
> *(Alan lights up, inhales deeply and passes it over.)*

EDDIE
> *(Inhaling deeply)*
> Lordie! Lordie!
> *(Takes hit, then another, and passes it back.)*

ALAN
> Acapulco gold, man. All the way from south of the border.
> *(Takes hit; passes it over)*

EDDIE
> *(Sings)*
> South of the border Down Mexico way...
> (Takes another hit)
> Bueno, bueno.

ALAN
> Muy bueno.

EDDIE
> *(Passing joint back)*
> Muchas gracias, Amigo. Muchas gracias.
> *(After killing fire, Alan saves joint, slumps into chair.)*
> Goodbye, Vermouth. Hello, Acapulco Gold.
> *(Beat)*
> You should introduce Hilda to our Mexican friend. It'll do her lotsa good getting stoned now and then.
> *(Alan says nothing.)*
> You might have to step down now that the man's (Tom) back.

ALAN
> *(Ignoring)*
> Rain, rain, go away...

EDDIE
It won't go away.

ALAN
...Little Eddie wants to play.

EDDIE
Tom and Hilda. Long before you came into the scene.

ALAN
Let it pour, let it pour...

EDDIE
You stepping down?

ALAN
(Singing)
I'm singing in the rain... Let it rain, let it rain, let it rain...

EDDIE
Thunderstorm and grass. Makes you hear weird things.

ALAN
Music, man. Music.

EDDIE
Shit-kicking country music?

ALAN
Tchaikovsky's Fifth.

EDDIE
Turn it down.
(When Alan simulates conductor's motions)
Will you turn the damn thing down!

ALAN
> *(Vigorously conducting)*
> Tchaikovsky, man! Tchaikovsky!

EDDIE
> *(Cupping ears)*
> Those drums!

ALAN
> *(Relenting)*
> How about some Gershwin?

EDDIE
> Yeah, man. Borgy and Bess
> *(Sings verse: "Don't know when...")*

TOM
> *(Stirs on couch, then suddenly jumps up, not knowing where he is. He sniffs.)*
> Fire! Fire!
> *(Alan and Eddie jump up.)*
> Fire!

EDDIE
> *(Rushing over)*
> Hey, Tom! Tom, baby! There's no fire.
> *(Tom stares at him.)*
> It's me, Eddie.
> *(Tom gazes around, gradually coming around.)*
> There's no fire, Tom.

TOM
> Then whydahell you yell fire for!
> *(Sitting back down in a stupor, reaches under couch for flask, and takes long pull.)*

EDDIE
> Bad nightmare, eh?

TOM
> I was deserted on an island.

EDDIE
> With Jap soldiers?

TOM
> With you and a bottle of Vermouth.

EDDIE
> Lucky me!

ALAN
> Want something to eat, Tom?

TOM
> Eat!

ALAN
> There's food in the ramada.

TOM
> *(Stares balefully at Alan, then to Eddie)*
> Where'd you find him?

EDDIE
> Him? He's our cook.

TOM
> He just burnt something.

EDDIE
> *(To Alan with Chinese accent)*

Hear that, Wong? Your cooking, no good, no good. Burn! Burn! Burn!

ALAN
Maybe, he wants a hit.

EDDIE
(To Tom)
Want a hit, Tom?

TOM
(Sniffs. To Alan.)
Where'd you get it? Vietnam? That war over there would've been over if you guys did less smoking and more fighting. Killed lotsa VCs?

ALAN
Some.

EDDIE
Hey, Tom, baby. C'mon. Have a hit.

TOM
I'm having a drink. A man's drink.
(Takes another pull)
Your great war novel, any combat in it?

ALAN
Some.

TOM
When there's no front lines there?!

ALAN
All of Nam is a front line.

TOM
   Don't tell me about it. I was there.

ALAN
   Yeah. You were there all right.

TOM
   In my war, we stood our grounds. The Japs as well as the Ameri-
   cans. A bucket of blood for every inch of ground gained or lost.

ALAN
   (Mimicking Churchill)
   "...Never in the history of mankind have so many owed so much
   to so few..."

TOM
   You're damn right! We never had it made like you punks had it
   over there.

ALAN
   Yeah. We sure had it made.

EDDIE
   That war of yours was some war, Tom. Alan's war?
   (Shrugs)

TOM
   So what's there to write about?

EDDIE
   The war that wasn't.

TOM
   Hear that, Kid? The war that wasn't.

ALAN
   You should know all about it.

TOM

   (On his feet)
   Hey, Eddie. Remember how I used to disarm you?

EDDIE

   Do I!

TOM

   (Takes out knife, offering)
   C'mon. Come for me with it.

EDDIE

   No way!

TOM

   (To Alan)
   How about you, Kid? C'mon.

ALAN

   (Mimicking)
   No way!

TOM

   *(Putting knife back into sheath, kneeling at coffee table, prepar-
   ing for arm wrestle)*
   C'mon, Eddie. I'll let you use both hands.

EDDIE

   Not with the champion of the world. No way.

TOM

   C'mon, Kid.

EDDIE

   Go on, Alan.

ALAN
  Naw.

TOM
  C'mon, Kid. You might get lucky.

ALAN
  (Finally)
  Well, okay...
  (They arm wrestle for a few seconds then, Alan, feigning weariness, gives in.)

TOM
  Pretty tough for an old timer, eh?

ALAN
  Yeah. You're tough all right.

EDDIE
  Let him use both hands, Tom.

TOM
  Want to, Kid?

ALAN
  Naw. You'll beat me again.
  (The door, Up Right, swings open and Hilda steps in with armful of vegetables. Dripping wet, she stares at three of them. Alan rises from floor, Eddie backs away; Tom remains on floor. Hilda disappears into kitchen as three of them wait anxiously.)

HILDA
  (Reappearing, controlling herself)
  Having a party?

TOM
  We've been waiting for you.

EDDIE
> My cabin's leaking.

ALAN
> So is mine.

HILDA
> *(Sniffs suspiciously. To Tom.)*
> What's wrong with your place?

TOM
> We happened to meet here.

HILDA
> Get out! All of you! Get out!

TOM
> Now wait-a-minute!
> *(Eddie and Alan cross to door, Up Right.)*

HILDA ·
> *(To Tom)*
> You ever smoke marijuana around here again so help me! I'll bash your goddamn head in!

EDDIE
> Mama. It wasn't him.

HILDA
> Get out of here before I...!
> *(Eddie and Alan rush out)*

TOM
> You should smoke it yourself. It'll do you some good.

HILDA
> You dope addict! You two-faced, doubling-crossing drunkard!

TOM

Now hold it! When did I ever double-cross you!

HILDA

When!

TOM

I left here because...

HILDA

I kicked you out!

TOM

I left!
(Beat)
—Aw, for Chrissake...

HILDA

Oh, no, you don't. You opened the gate.

TOM

Will you stop this crap!

HILDA

You started to believe all the...crap about what a great writer you are. Look what it got you!

TOM

Now don't start that shit about making a writer out of me. I was a writer long before you came along.

HILDA

Ha!

TOM

Whattahell you "ha-ing" about, you old bat!

HILDA
You couldn't write a decent sentence then, and you still can't!

TOM
I can outwrite every one of you with only half my brain working, and you know it.

HILDA
(Stepping over to bookshelf, pulling out books)
You call this writing!
(Throws book at Tom.)
And this!
(Also throws it at him.)
And this! Trash! Garbage! Every one of them! You didn't have sense enough to get out of the rain when I took you in, and you still don't!

TOM
You took me in because you wanted a young stud and I happened to be around.

HILDA
You bum! You fiddlefucking shithead bum! Get out of here! Get out! And don't you ever step foot in my cabin again!

TOM
(Stepping to door, Up Left, stops. Relenting)
For Chrissake, Hilda...

HILDA
(Throwing book)
Get out!

TOM
(Finally leaving)
Goddamn old bat...
(Hilda stares at door. In a moment, she picks up books and wipes

them delicately, fondly. Lights begin to dim until)

BLACKOUT

Act Two, Scene I

(Next day. Noon. We HEAR singing and chirping of birds and clacking of a typewriter. As lights brighten, Hilda is at her desk busy working on her novel. She pulls out paper from typewriter, reads it, then unsatisfied, crumbles it and heaves it into wastebasket. Placing another paper into typewriter, she starts all over. In a moment)

EDDIE (O.S.)
Mama. Mama Thatcher.

HILDA
Come in, Eddie.

EDDIE
(Stepping in, cautiously)
Your note on my door, it said you wanted to see me.

HILDA
(Indicating chair beside her)
Sit down.
(Reaches for chapter of Eddie's novel.)

EDDIE
(Sitting uneasily)
My typewriter ribbon, it acted up again. But I got it fixed.

HILDA
(Going through notes)
Good.

EDDIE

Mama, last night, it wasn't Tom's fault.
(Hilda glances up; continues reading.)
We were all waiting for you and...

HILDA

Forget about last night.

EDDIE

—Oh, I already did.
(Beat)
The days seem so long getting up at sunrise. Nothing to do after you're through writing.

HILDA

Start jogging.

EDDIE

Jogging! I did all the running I ever want to do growing up in St. Louis. Running away from the cops, running away from the school teachers, running away from the rednecks always wanting to kick my nigger ass. Is that what you wanted to tell me? Start jogging?

HILDA

I want to talk to you about this chapter.

EDDIE

It's awful, isn't it? I don't know what ever made me think you'd like it. Let me rewrite it, Mama.

HILDA

Let's go over it first.

EDDIE

It's not worth it.

HILDA

Will you shut up, for God's sake!

EDDIE

That bad, eh?

HILDA

It's great!

EDDIE

It is?! Oh, I knew you'd like it. I just knew it.

HILDA

It needs more work. But it's all there. Very poignant. Very moving. The weakness is the author's bitterness.

EDDIE

I'm not bitter anymore.

HILDA

It shows. You shouldn't let it get between you and your characters. You have to be more detached. More discerning.

EDDIE

I don't hate those people anymore. I pity them.

HILDA

Don't even pity them. Understand them. Become them. Utterly. Like you did with all the characters in your first book.
(Beat)
Be grateful for all you've been through, Eddie. It sensitized you to the miseries and suffering of others. It made you what you are today.

EDDIE

I owe it all to you, Mama.

HILDA
(Shaking head)
We take a little; we give a little, Eddie. You've learned from me; I've learned from you. Until you came along I never really knew a negro.

EDDIE
—A black.

HILDA
A black. Who is an extraordinarily talented writer.

EDDIE
I owe you my life, Mama.

HILDA
Stop that! You owe it to yourself to become the great writer you're going to be. Can't you see, Dear. You always had it in you. All I did was make you aware of it.

EDDIE
(Embracing)
Oh, Mama. I love you so much.

HILDA
(Embracing with great warmth)
And I shall always love you, Dear.

TOM
(Slightly drunk, enters, Up Left, with envelope.)
Hey, Hilda. A telegram for that great writer of yours.

HILDA
Telegram?
(Rushing to Tom)
For Alan?

TOM
(Handing)
A kid brought it over.

HILDA
(Takes telegram, reads envelope. Quickly crosses over to door, Up Right.)
Alan! Alan!

EDDIE
(To Tom)
Who's it from?

TOM
(Shrugging)
Who knows.

HILDA
It's from New York.

EDDIE
From Rasmussen?

HILDA
It must be.
(Through screen door again)
Alan! Alan!

ALAN (O.S.)
What's the matter?

HILDA
(Through door)
This just came for you.

ALAN
(Enters. Apprehensively)
A...telegram? From home?

HILDA
(Handing)
From New York.

ALAN
Christ. I thought something happened back home.
(Opens envelope.)
Holy shit!

HILDA
Who is it from?

ALAN
Wow!

HILDA
Alan!

ALAN
It's from Rasmussen.
(Jubilantly)
He sold my story!
(Hugging Hilda)
He sold my story! He sold it!

HILDA
Let me see that! Alan! Let me see it!
(Reads)
He did it! Oliver sold it!
(Hugs Alan)
Oh, Alan! You've done it! And Hilton Publishing!

EDDIE
(Taking telegram)
You did it!
(Embracing Alan)
You did it, man!

ALAN
I'm going to be published!

EDDIE
Hell, yeah, man!

HILDA
I knew it! I just knew it would be accepted.

ALAN
(Hugging Hilda again)
I owe it all to you. Everything! I love you! I love you!
(Kisses her, then backs away, awkwardly, aware that Tom is watching.)

TOM
(Finally; half-heartedly)
Congratulations, Kid. —I mean it.

ALAN
Thanks, Tom.

HILDA
(To Tom)
Hilton Publishing.

TOM
Hilton, eh?

ALAN
My first novel.

TOM
I know exactly how you feel, Kid. Nothing like it in the whole
world, having your first novel accepted.

ALAN
I...still can't believe it.

WRITINGS FROM THE HANDY COLONY

TOM

You will, Kid. You will. Especially when you see your name on the jacket.

HILDA

(To Tom)
Remember when you received your first telegram?

TOM

Do I?
(Takes flask out, drinks.)

HILDA

They were willing to give you an advance even before you finished your story.

TOM

Yeah, we sure celebrated. Went up to Chicago for couple of days. Then to New York to meet the publisher and the editor.

EDDIE

Where's the champagne, Mama?

TOM

Hell, yeah, Hilda. Champagne for everybody.

ALAN

Why don't we all go over to Terre Haute?

EDDIE

I hear you!

HILDA

You go ahead. All of you.

ALAN

Don't you want to go?

EDDIE

C'mon, Mama. It's celebration time.

HILDA

Go on. Have a nice time.

EDDIE

Aw, Mama.

TOM

(Drinks from flask.)
I think I'll stick around.

EDDIE

Man! Since when you turn down an invitation to a party?

TOM

You guys go ahead.

EDDIE

(Heading, Up Right)
C'mon, Alan.

ALAN

(Hesitating, looks at Tom, at Hilda; finally to Eddie)
Maybe, we should do it some other time.

HILDA

Go on, Alan.

EDDIE

C'mon, man.

ALAN

(To Hilda)
You sure you don't want to come along?

HILDA
I'll wait until your book comes out. Then, we'll really celebrate.

TOM
Hell, yeah.

ALAN
(Studies Tom.)
Well, okay, then.
(Kisses Hilda.)
Thank you, Hilda. For everything.

HILDA
You deserve it, Dear. Every bit of it.

ALAN
Well, we'll see you later.
(Heads Up Right, looks back at Hilda, at Tom, and finally exits with Eddie.)

HILDA
His first novel! Isn't that exciting?

TOM
(Toasting)
Here's to the birth of your latest writer.

HILDA
(Beat)
How long are you going to keep it up?

TOM
It's an occasion, remember?

HILDA
An ant race is an occasion to you.

TOM

>A personal triumph for you, too. Where would the kid be without you? Where...would we all be without you.

HILDA

>*(Mimicking)*
>"You wanted a young stud and I happened to be around."

TOM

>Aw, "hogwash."

HILDA

>As long as you're going to keep drinking, do it at your own place.

TOM

>For Chrissake, Hilda... All we've been doing since yesterday is getting at each other's throat. Can't we talk?

HILDA

>*(Looks at him.)*
>All right.
>*(Sits in chair.)*
>This is as good a time as any.
>*(Calculatingly)*
>You have the right of first refusal.

TOM

>First refusal?

HILDA

>To buy me out.

TOM

>Why...would I want to do that?

HILDA

>If you don't want to, I'll talk to Spencer Hoyt.

TOM
> You want to sell out?

HILDA
> Don't you?

TOM
> Well... If that's what you want. Where will you go?

HILDA
> Oh, I don't know. Arizona, California, New Mexico. I just want to get away and live a life of my own for a change.

TOM
> What about them? Alan? Eddie?

HILDA
> They'll be all right. They've learned to believe in themselves. God knows that's half the battle. You going back to New York?

TOM
> Yeah. Maybe.
> *(Beat)*
> I might go down to Florida.

HILDA
> Fishing?

TOM
> *(Nodding)*
> And do some serious writing. I used to write pretty good down there. Remember?

HILDA
> *(Challengingly)*
> It's been a long time, Tom.

TOM

I'll buy me a shack near the beach and really get down to business.

HILDA

It won't be easy.

TOM

I can still outwrite the best of them. Including that boy wonder of yours.

HILDA

He's coming out with a great one.

TOM

I'll come out with a greater one!

HILDA

That'll take some doing.

TOM

You sure believe in me, don't you?

HILDA

As much as you believe in yourself.

TOM

(Beat)

Maybe, I'll take a trip to the South Pacific. Always wanted to return there.

HILDA

I'm sure there's room for another *Return to Paradise*.

TOM

(Beat)

I might even go to Paris or...to Africa.

HILDA

I'm sure Hemingway didn't say all there is to say about Kilimanjaro.

TOM

Aw, those lousy foreign places. I might see you in Arizona, or California, or New Mexico.

HILDA

Be sure to bring your wife and daughter along.

TOM

You know goddamn well we're not together anymore.

HILDA

Come to think of it, Eddie did mention it.

TOM

(Beat)
The marriage was doomed even before we... When the baby came along... —Anyway, the divorce was final over a year ago. I gave her everything. The house, the car, the bank account. Even the rights to my books. They'll be all right.

HILDA

That's good to know.

TOM

(Drinks last drop in flask, and heaves flask away. Rising)
That's it! No more! Finito!

HILDA

Be sure to have a clear head for tomorrow's meeting with old man Hoyt.

TOM

(Stepping, Up Left)
That toadhead... That goddamn creep.

HILDA

Remember. We want the best deal we can get.

TOM

(Exiting)
Sonsofbitches... It's always them and us.
(Hilda crosses Right and picks up flask. Shakes it. Empty. She glances toward mansion. Lights begin dimming, until)

BLACKOUT

ACT TWO, SCENE II

(Same scene. Late that afternoon. Hilda is at chair mending a jogging outfit. After a moment, Tom enters, Up Left. He has a horrendous hangover and looks it, his eyes bloodshot, his hair disheveled, his clothes wrinkled, his movements unsteady and uncertain.)

HILDA

(As Tom crosses toward her and slumps on couch)
Couldn't sleep?

TOM

(Dying for a drink)
What time is it?

HILDA

Five-thirty.

TOM

Yesterday or tomorrow?

HILDA

There's a fresh pot of coffee on the stove.

TOM
In a second.

HILDA
You'll feel better.

TOM
I said, in a second.
(Hilda glances at him, not without sympathy.)
...Not among the living yet.

HILDA
(Showing jogging pants)
Looks familiar to you?

TOM
Your pajamas?

HILDA
Your jogging pants.

TOM
Where'd you find it?

HILDA
In my closet. I'm taking in the waistline. You lost a little weight
since you left.

TOM
Among other things.

HILDA
You should go on a fast. Then start jogging down the beach and
get lots of exercise.

TOM
Beach?

HILDA

Down in Florida. Near that shack you plan to buy.
(Tom looks at her.)
I'm going to start jogging, too.

TOM

Who're you planning on fighting?

HILDA

(Ignoring)
I was going to start today, but I have to leave.

TOM

You're leaving?

HILDA

Harry, Florence's husband, died last week. —You remember Harry.

TOM

Harry Campbell died? Oh, yeah. Yeah, he did, didn't he?

HILDA

I told Florence I'd be down again today.
(Beat)
In a way, it was a blessing.

TOM

I should have the same blessing.

HILDA

How else do you expect to feel after...?

TOM

—Goddamnit! That's the last thing I need right now. An AA session.

HILDA

(Pause. She continues mending; Tom stares at nothing.)

What's your next book going to be about?
(Tom says nothing)
No idea?
(Tom remains silent)
How about a sequel to *Above and Beyond*?

TOM
   (Rising)
   I need some coffee.
   (Crosses into kitchen)

HILDA
   We talked about it, remember?

TOM (O.S.)
   Yeah, we did.

HILDA
   Ever mention it to your publisher?
   (Beat)
   Tom?
   (Beat)
   The cups are on the top shelf.
   (Beat)
   Tom?

TOM (O.S.)
   Yeah. Got it.

HILDA
   (Tom reappears and crosses back to couch, coffee cup shaking.)
   I made it nice and strong.

TOM
   (Sips, relishing coffee medicinally)
   Exactly what I need.

HILDA

I think a sequel would be very timely now.

TOM

I already wrote it.

HILDA

You did?

TOM

(Beat)
It was rejected.

HILDA

Rejected!

TOM

By Mereweather. At Hilton.
(Hilda looks at him as he sips again, the coffee, somehow, helping him to recover rather rapidly.)
That sonofabitch. I made him millions and he suddenly decides another novel on the Pacific War won't sell.

HILDA

You had it taking place during the war?

TOM

The war was still on when *A and B* ended.

HILDA

The war is over and done with as far as the sequel is concerned. It's post-war now. Everyone is readjusting.

TOM

I had to show what happened to my guys the last days of the war.

HILDA
Tom. People are just not interested in a war that happened over twenty-five years ago.

TOM
They would be if they knew what we went through.

HILDA
We're involved in another war now. And it's no longer "My country right or wrong."
(Crosses to bookshelf, Left, pulls out a book and hands it.)
Here. Go back and read *A and B* carefully. Especially the second half.

TOM
I wrote the damn thing!

HILDA
Find a way to ease your characters into another era.

TOM
(Picking up cup)
I need another cup.
(Crosses into kitchen.)

HILDA
Was someone editing your stuff?

TOM (O.S.)
I did it myself.

HILDA
(Mutters)
That figures...

TOM (O.S.)
Two years! It took me two goddamn years to write it.

HILDA

It took you over five years to write *Above and Beyond*.

TOM (O.S.)

I wrote every day, seven days a week.

HILDA

You should have gotten someone to look it over as you went along.

TOM

(Reappearing with cup, now much less hungover.)
You really think I should've stayed away from the war?

HILDA

Utterly.

TOM

(sips)
The agent thinks Cosmic might take it.

HILDA

The paperback company?

TOM

I can use the money.

HILDA

The sequel should be rewritten.

TOM

I'm broke.

HILDA

(Avoiding his eyes)
Not after tomorrow.

TOM

I'm not having two whole years go down the drain.

HILDA

You went down the drain the day you started writing all that trash for TV and movies.

TOM

I stopped writing all that crap once I started the sequel.

HILDA

And your wife, of course, missed the income needed to keep up with all her New York and Hollywood friends.

TOM

(Ignoring, sips more coffee.)
Remember the time I went AWOL in San Francisco and found myself passed out at Fisherman's Wharf? Well, this time it was Greenwich Village.

HILDA

And it wasn't returning to camp, but here?

TOM

Where I still have a place to hang my hat.

HILDA

For a few days anyway.

TOM

(Pause)
Whydahell don't you say it?
(Hilda looks at him.)
Goddamnit! Say it!

HILDA

You always wanted to experience that New York life, Tom.

TOM

I got creamed back there. And you know it.

HILDA

(Looks at him tenderly, affectionately, then catching herself)
—There! Finished.
(Showing jogging pants)
It should fit you perfectly now.

TOM

Nothing like perfectly fitting jogging pants.

HILDA

(Placing pants on couch)
I have to leave.

TOM

Right now?!

HILDA

I'm already late.
(Crosses, Up Right.)

TOM

We've got lots to talk about.

HILDA

(At door, looking back)
Yes. I'm sure we do.
(Exits. Tom steps into kitchen; comes out with bottle. He pours into cup and drinks whiskey-coffee as he apparently had been doing all along. He picks up flask and pours whiskey into it. Lights gradually begin to dim.)

BLACKOUT

ACT TWO, SCENE III

(Same scene. That night, a few hours later. Hilda enters from kitchen with half-empty bottle. She studies it, not quite sure whether it was Alan and Eddie or Tom. She looks out at the mansion, then Up Right, toward the writers' cabin. As she steps back into kitchen to put bottle back, we HEAR a car pulling up outside, slamming of car doors, and:)

ALAN (O.S.)
Yeah, right... We'll see you in the morning...

EDDIE (O.S.)
(Singing verse from Porgy and Bess, *drunkenly, voice fading distantly)*

ALAN (O.S.)
(Imitating Eddie's singing, approaching door)
Hilda. Hilda!
(Enters, Up Right, with bouquet of flowers. Quite drunk, he is still exuberant.)
Hilda.

HILDA
(Appearing from kitchen)
Hi, Alan.

ALAN
Oh. There you are.

HILDA
How long have you been back?

ALAN
Just drove in.

HILDA

(*Looks toward mansion, knowing it was Tom, after all, who drank from bottle.*)
Had a nice time?

ALAN

(*Imitating Eddie*)
"...Screaming, bubbling, ass-kicking time..."
(*Offering flowers*)
Here. For you.

HILDA

Oh, thank you, Alan. They're beautiful. You shouldn't be spending money you haven't gotten yet.

ALAN

The money from the book, they're all yours.

HILDA

(*Stepping toward kitchen with flowers*)
If you want to, you can donate some of it to the Colony. To help other writers.

ALAN

That's what I'll do. Donate it all to the Colony.

HILDA (O.S.)

Not all. Just a portion.

ALAN

You think they'll make a movie outta my book?

HILDA (O.S.)

I'm sure the agent is already working on it.

ALAN

You really think so?

God! I've been dreaming about all this so long I keep feeling it's nothing but a goddamn dream.

HILDA
(Reappearing with flowers in vase)
Here. Smell these.
(Alan does.)
Still think it's just a dream?

ALAN
(Smells again. Poetically)
...From the abysmal depth of a cesspool to a radiant garden of roses... —And I owe it all to you! "Utterly."
(Hugs Hilda.)
Oh, how I love you!
(Lifts her.)
I love you, Hilda!

HILDA
Alan!

ALAN
I love you, Hilda! I love you!

HILDA
Alan! Put me down!

ALAN
Not until you tell me you love me, too.

HILDA
Alan!

ALAN
(Finally relenting)
I wish you had gone with us.

That Eddie, he kept telling everyone in the bar about my book. —
And about the colony.

HILDA

> That's our Eddie.

ALAN

> There was this waitress...

HILDA

> Uh huh...

ALAN

> She once submitted something to you, she said.

HILDA

> From Terre Haute?

ALAN

> From Terre Haute. She said you told her she wasn't ready to come
> to the Colony.

HILDA

> Most of them are not.

ALAN

> She wanted to become a writer so badly she even went to live in
> New York.

HILDA

> Did she get published?

ALAN

> She gave it all up. Just couldn't take the rejections.

HILDA

> Most of them can't.

ALAN

Won't it be something, your book and mine coming out the same time?

HILDA

Yes. Yes, that would be something.

ALAN

Oh, Hilda. I know it will. I just know it.
(Beat)
Hilda, let's get married.
(Hilda is startled.)
Let's get married, Hilda. Tomorrow!

HILDA

You did have a lot to drink.

ALAN

I'm not drunk. Just happy. Ecstatically. And I wanna share it with you. Forever.

HILDA

We'll always share our happiness, Alan.

ALAN

Then, you will marry me?

HILDA

(Shaking head, emphatically)
No.

ALAN

Why not? Now, I don't wanna hear about the difference in our age. 'Cause that's a crock of shit.

HILDA

I would be less than honest if I said it had nothing to do with it.

ALAN
 We already went through all that!

HILDA
 Alan...

ALAN
 It was meant to be!

HILDA
 Alan!
 (Beat)
 How long will it take you to finish that chapter you're working on?

ALAN
 Another week. Maybe, two.

HILDA
 I want you to leave when you're finished.

ALAN
 Leave? For where?

HILDA
 For home. For wherever you want to go to finish your next book.

ALAN
 You're sending me away?

HILDA
 You can send me your chapters like you use to.

ALAN
 It's 'cause of him (Tom), isn't it?
 (Hilda says nothing)
 You're sending me away 'cause of that drunkard! That arrogant, obnoxious sonofabitch!

How can you go back to him after what he's done to you?!

HILDA

He needs help.

ALAN

He's about to sell you out!

HILDA

He's back because this is where he does his best writing.

ALAN

Can't you see? Can't you see what he's doing? To you? To me? To us?

HILDA

I owe it to him.

ALAN

You owe him nothing!

HILDA

(Shaking head)
Until he came along, I was just another English teacher in a small
country high school. After his books came out...
And all I really did was to make him believe in himself.

ALAN

He's turned out to be nothing but an ungrateful, backstabbing,
slobbering drunkard!

HILDA

He's a different person when he's not drinking. In a way, you two
are very much alike. Excesses. Never moderation. You're either
drunk or you're not. When he made all that money from his first
book, he wanted to give it all to me to start a writers colony. To
help other writers like yourself get started.

ALAN

He's not helping me. You are.

HILDA

(Shakes head)
Everything out there, the cabins, the swimming pool, the stacks of books in the library, the ramada kitchen... That was all his idea. His money.

ALAN

I'm gonna buy him out. He'll get back every penny.

HILDA

You owe him nothing. I do.

ALAN

(Beat)
What's gonna happen to us? To you and me?

HILDA

We'll always be together. Utterly. In our thoughts. In our spirit. In everything we do. What we've shared—and will continue to share—will be with us even after we're gone. In the garden that we spoke of many times.

ALAN

Hilda. We need each other. You said so yourself.
(The door, Up Left, suddenly swings open, and Tom staggers in.)

TOM

ATTENTION!
(Quite drunk, he is in World War II combat outfit, helmet, pistol, bayonet, boots with leggings, old fatigue jacket with sergeant's stripes. Startled, Hilda and Alan stare.)
At ease.
(Drinks from flask; crosses to Alan.)
ATTENTION! You heard me, soldier! ATTENTION!

(Alan steps away, refusing to go along.)
You are out of order, soldier! You are out of order!
(To Hilda)
Corporal! You will see to it that this man is restricted to quarters until further orders. Furthermore, you will see to it that this man is thoroughly familiar with the Military Code of Justice regarding respect for his superiors.

HILDA
(Scornfully)
To his superiors, yes.

TOM
(Breaks; grinning)
You gotta admit. I would've been a helluva general.

HILDA
For the enemy.

TOM
(To Alan)
I would've shown you guys what combat is all about.

ALAN
Yeah. Sure.

TOM
We would've wiped 'em out. Every one of them bastards! What you guys going through over there, it's no war. It's a maneuver to what we went through.

ALAN
Yeah. Sure.

TOM
In my war we obeyed; we did not question. We fought and died; we did not cry and run.

ALAN

> And no one's dying in this war!?

TOM

> War? It's a picnic.

ALAN

> *(Exploding)*
> Whattahell you know what's going on over there! You never even got out of Saigon!

HILDA

> Alan. Go back to your cabin.

ALAN

> Not until I tell this...war monger...!
> *(Raising his shirt, shows hideous scar.)*
> This looks like I got it in a maneuver!
> *(Lifting pants leg)*
> This looks like I got it in a picnic! You and your goddamn war!

HILDA

> *(Urging Alan to leave)*
> Alan!

ALAN

> *(At door)*
> Anytime you wanna arm wrestle me again, just let me know. I'll let you use both hands. —And both feet!
> *(Exits)*

TOM

> Whattahell's the matter with him? Acts like a dog chasing his own tail.

HILDA

> *(Surveying Tom's outfit)*
> Think the Japs are going to invade Creighton?

TOM

I went on a twenty-mile hike.

HILDA

And got thirsty? What happened to, "That's it! No more! Finito!"

TOM

Who told you to keep that damn bottle in the kitchen!?

HILDA
(Wearily)
You do whatever you want to do, Tom.

TOM

You're feeling all right?

HILDA

As all right as you are.

TOM

Howdahell would you know how I'm feeling? They accept that kid's book. And turned me down. Me! Tom Wilson!
(Slumps in chair.)
...Never even bothered to call me.
(Quotes)
"...We have decided that your novel is not suitable for our market at this time...." A note from his secretary.

HILDA
(Sympathizing)
You'll bounce back, Tom. You will.

TOM

I don't know if there's any more bounces left in me. It's a jungle out there, Hilda. No rules; no mercy; no holds barred. A bunch of heartless, merciless motherfucking animals! Utterly!

HILDA
(Stepping toward kitchen)
Why don't you finish the bottle.

TOM
I can't get any drunker.

HILDA
You sure you're all right?

TOM
Never better under the circumstance, Hilda Thatcher. Never better.
(Steps to door, Up Left, stops. Recites)
The time has come to take my leave
And amble on home to my last retreat
The day is done and I now believe
All is well on the dark lonely street.
(Looks at Hilda, then exists.)

HILDA
Tom...
(Stands there, tempted. Finally, crosses Down Right to desk, and stands there looking at her manuscript, the specter of a possible rejection haunting her. Picking up manuscript, holds it fondly. Suddenly, we HEAR a loud BANG! from the mansion. Hilda drops manuscript, dashes Up Left. Halts. She stands there, frozen, holding her ground. Stepping over to window, looks toward the mansion, prayerfully. Seconds later, Eddie, then Alan, rush in, Up right.)

EDDIE
Mama! You all right?!

ALAN
Where did that come from?!

HILDA
(Indicating mansion)
Over there.

EDDIE
Tom's!

ALAN
(Rushing Up Left with Eddie)
Holy shit!

HILDA
Alan! Eddie!
(They halt)

EDDIE
He could've...!

ALAN
He might be...!

HILDA
He's all right.

EDDIE
Mama!

ALAN
We better go over, Hilda.

HILDA
He's all right!
(The door, Up Left, slowly opens and Tom staggers in. Hilda looks away, relieved. Now, seemingly indifferent)
Your gun misfired?

TOM
> (*Studies three of them*)
> Then...you heard it?

HILDA
> Did you expect us not to?

TOM
> I could've been dying!

HILDA
> You? Tom Wilson? An expert marksman?

TOM
> (*To Alan and Eddie*)
> Fine friends you guys turned out to be.

EDDIE
> Tom. We knew you were all right.

TOM
> My buddies.

ALAN
> Christ, Tom.

TOM
> (*To Hilda*)
> And you! You'd let me bleed to death!

HILDA
> Just as long as it's not in my cabin.

TOM
> You bitch!

HILDA

You fiddlefucking gutless cesspool! Get out of here! Get out! I want fighters around me! Not whimpering cry babies!

TOM

I'll show you who's a fighter, you old windbag! I'll show you I'm still the best writer around!

HILDA

You! You don't know a period from a comma!

TOM

I can outwrite all of you put together! And you know goddamn well I can!

HILDA

You're exactly what Spencer Hoyt said you are. A flashin-the-pan!

TOM

He said that! That fuckhead! He said that! You tell him he steps foot on my property I'll skin him alive!
(Stepping toward, Up Left)
A flash-in-the-pan, eh? I'll show him. I'll show all of you!
(At door)
You haven't heard the last of Tom Wilson! Not by a long shot!

HILDA

(Door closes behind Tom, and a triumphant smile creeps up Hilda's face. To Eddie and Alan who are stunned by the savage exchange)
Someday, when you get a rejection, you'll know what he's going through.

ALAN

Rejection?

EDDIE

Tom got a rejection? Oh, man. I better go over...

HILDA
   Eddie!

EDDIE
   (Halting)
   But, Mama...!

HILDA
   He's going to be all right.

ALAN
   All those lousy things I said to him...

HILDA
   He knows we're all pulling for him.
   (Beat)
   You better go back to your cabin.

EDDIE
   (Crossing, Up Right, stopping)
   You're going to be all right, Mama?

HILDA
   Yes, Dear. I'm going to be fine. Just fine.
   (Eddie exits. As Alan steps toward door)
   Alan. I want you to leave in the morning.

ALAN
   Tomorrow morning?!

HILDA
   (Nodding)
   As early as you can.

ALAN
   Hilda. He might leave in a day or two.

HILDA
(Shaking head)
He'll be his old self in a few days. He'll be writing again.

ALAN
Do I get to see you before I leave?

HILDA
Let's not make it any more difficult than we have to.
(They look at each other. Finally, Alan steps over to door, then fighting himself, exits. Hilda stands there looking at door. She now crosses Down Right and picks up manuscript on floor. She holds the manuscript fondly, and steps over to fireplace. She stands there a long moment, the manuscript close to her. She begins to tear the pages and drops them into the fire. Lights gradually dim until)

CURTAIN

Extracts from a May 19, 1964, letter to Jon Shirota from Lowney Handy

May 19, 1964

Dear Jon:

It seems that I have achieved, unknowingly myself, the thing I usually have to achieve with all writers, actually, the sooner, the better for them...and that is a freedom.

The writer is frightened, and clings to the known, hopes and believes until he is imprisoned by his hopes.

The Handy Colony is a wall, is safe as your mother's apron-string, which you abhorred in Maui, and would equally abhor if I allowed you to hang yourself by it.

Following something I learned the very hard way, I steeled myself to your fears, and you seeking my warmth of encouragement, for someday you would resent the things it would take from you.

Instead I have made you walk...and never crawl....

The secret is to offer as little hope as possible, the writer has such an abundance that he will cheat himself, in the exuberant and self-praise of his own enthusiasm.

I think you will at last understand the method of my working.

I leave you alone to do as much as you can.

You must stop feeling that something you have done or have not done has offended me. I AM NOT GOD. And I am not offended. I am your friend, who by withholding too many things, may help you to achieve your first and greatest dream. I THINK YOU WILL. I think you are over the hump. I know it hasn't been easy, but you have crossed a bridge....

Another thing. It is good to make a journey, before you do that first draft—AND TO MAKE ANOTHER JOURNEY—or even write on something else before you do the next draft. You have learned how to write.

I BELIEVE COMPLETELY AND ULTIMATELY IN YOUR GREATNESS.

Much love, and of course we can always meet IN THE GARDEN...when you build a garden anyone who knows the way can come. I have never seen the Colony as beautiful [as it is] this year....

—*Courtesy of Jon Shirota*

*[This is the last letter Lowney wrote to Jon, who was planning to be at the Colony during the summer. Lowney, however, died in June 1964. —*EDS.*]*

AFTERWORD

As this collection of previously unpublished writings from the Handy Colony reaffirm, there has been nothing like it on the American literary landscape. Just as the mute traces of the Colony buildings and grounds still form a legible outcropping at the edge of Marshall, Illinois, so these prose remnants of the Colony's founder and followers testify to the vitality of their shared, it short-lived, vision.

Neither the Colony nor the work it nurtured would have existed without Lowney Handy, its tutelary spirit. Unencumbered by the usual credentials of college degree or publication record, she attracted students by her supreme confidence that everyone had a story worth telling and that she could teach them how to tell it so the world would listen. If, in the end, she proved unable to practice what she preached, and thus never produced publishable fiction of her own, she nevertheless took pardonable pride in the performance of her ablest protégés.

Like the first and foremost of these disciples, James Jones, most of the Handy colonists were literary long shots when they sought Lowney's guidance and support. Whereas other writers' colonies required applicants to present their bonafides for admission, Lowney preferred to mentor neophytes who were less likely to challenge her unorthodox approach. If her pupils had been knocked around by life during and after WWII, she supplied the regimen—part military, part monastic—by which they could win redemption. And when they enjoyed success, they were quick to credit her influence.

To read the rich, revealing sample of materials assembled here, from Lowney's own story and letters to recollections as well as fiction by several colonists, is to confront anew the mystery of the creative process. What, precisely, was Lowney's contribution to the writing of her pupils? Was she muse or midwife, angel or albatross? While the evidence resists a definitive answer, it does suggest her generous gift of the four things Herman Melville identified as necessary for the successful writer: "time, strength, cash, and patience."

TIME: Colonists wrote from 5:30 a.m. to noon seven days a week, with no holidays. Lowney patrolled the compound to make sure their typewriters were clacking. She made newcomers spend most of the morning copying word for word the works of great American realists like Hemingway. Only when a writer had progressed to her satisfaction was he permitted to work on his own manuscript. New writers showed up regularly, often after corresponding with Lowney, who sometimes even sent them bus tickets to Marshall. Once accepted, colonists were largely cut off from the outside world: newspapers, magazines, radios were forbidden. Lack of distraction assured long stretches of time for reflection and revision.

STRENGTH: Meals at the colony were ample, not memorable. Instant coffee and toast for breakfast; potatoes, corn on the cob, cottage cheese, and meat for lunch and dinner; Jello for dessert. No milk, butter, eggs. No alcohol, except for Jones, who drank double martinis to unknot his stomach. Lowney believed rich food hindered creativity, and she prescribed enemas for writer's block. She read daily what every colonist wrote and scribbled feedback in the margins, attacking the influence of authors she found precious or homosexual (like Eliot, Lawrence and Proust). As Jones explained in a 1956 letter, she was able to infuse her students with "confidence and enthusiasm, even when she is riding their ass," which gives them *"belief,* so hard to come by anywhere else."

CASH: The Handys supported the Colony generously. Harry contributed four hundred dollars a month from his salary as superintendent of the Ohio Oil Refinery in nearby Robinson. The Colony was built on a five-acre plot owned by his family, and refinery workers helped to construct the barracks where the writers worked and slept. Lowney even funded the monthly visits by male colonists to the brothels of Terre Haute, Indiana, across the Wabash River—excursions she viewed as essential, if regrettable, safety valves. In 1952 Jones gave sixty-five thousand dollars of his *From Here to Eternity* royalties to the Colony as repayment for the Handys' support after his discharge from the Army in 1944.

WRITINGS FROM THE HANDY COLONY

PATIENCE: According to John Bowers, two of Lowney's pet metaphors were the classical myth of the Phoenix and the Biblical story of faith as a mustard seed. In his memoir, Bowers recalls Lowney's advice to a faltering writer: All he needed was "the faith of a mustard seed" in order to be great. Such greatness, however, must come at the cost of his old self. "Kill that ego," she urged, "then rise from your dead ashes like the Phoenix bird." Jones, the former infantryman whom she had torn down and rebuilt, was proof that her precepts worked. Copy the right authors and eschew the rest, eat the prescribed diet, purge yourself of old ideas and bad habits, avoid romantic entanglements, and you too can write the great American novel.

Given the similar background of most colonists, and the persistent philosophy behind their instruction, we should not be surprised by two aspects of the Colony's twenty-year track record: first, that because many of Lowney's apprentices lacked the crucial ingredient she could *not* supply—namely talent—most of them failed to achieve artistic recognition; second, that whatever their personal abilities, they reflect in varying degrees the impact of Lowney's methods and models, both for better and for worse.

Confirming the maxim that those who can, do and those who can't, teach, Lowney's story strikes us as the weakest of the lot because—as those who knew her say—she never found a fictional equivalent for the fresh, forceful voice of her conversation and correspondence (this makes the inclusion of her letters in the present volume especially welcome). By contrast, in another illustration of the Handys' unique partnership, one often marked by role reversal, Harry's chapter is surprisingly strong, particularly in its implied comparison between the hero's turbulent work life and tendency to tell rather than to show flouts a lesson of the master that Harry had absorbed: suggestion can be more powerful than explicit (over) statement.

Underlying most of this newly available work is the belief that in a repressive society, individuality emerges most clearly in the heat of argument or the throes of passion. John Bowers, with several volumes of fiction and nonfiction to his credit, is the most polished stylist represented here, yet his preoccupations in "Long Gone in Tennessee" echo those of the rest. Don Sackrider's army story displays a sure dramatic sense while deploying a carefully crafted vernacular. The tantalizing summary of Mary Ann Jones' fragmentary novel reads like a companion piece to her brother's undervalued epic, *Some Came Running*, with which it shares both a contempt for small-town hypocrisy and a celebration of rebellion, however doomed.

The Last Retreat, Jon Shirota's elegy for the Colony and its complex, often contradictory leader, constitutes the perfect coda for the collection. Who better than the last colonist to portray, in retrospect, Lowney's combative relations with various versions of the masculine artistic temperament and the high price paid by all for the sublimation of her own creative impulses to the service of theirs?

As Shirota benefits from hindsight, so can we. It now seems clear, ironically, that the same qualities Lowney admired in the work of certain contemporary authors and urged her pupils to emulate in their own fiction simultaneously helped the best of them to break into print as latter-day realists, while limited their long-term critical appeal during the subsequent ascendancy of modernism. Whether these literary fashions and fortunes reverse in the future or not, *Writings from the Handy Colony* reminds us of a bygone era, like a historic marker that preserves the vanishing past for our eventual reconsideration. For this, we owe the editors and publisher a vote of thanks.

—Judith Everson and J. Michael Lennon

ACKNOWLEDGMENTS

We wish to thank Dr. Jim Turner, Lowney Turner Handy's nephew, for permission to quote parts of Harry Handy's *Turnaround*. That manuscript is now on loan to the Rare Book Room and Special Collections Library of the University of Illinois at Urbana-Champaign. The Library has also given us permission to reproduce parts of that novel.

From his personal collection, Don Sackrider provided copies of Lowney's story "V for Victory"; his own stories, "To Spite Your Own Face" and "Ode to the West"; copies of Lowney's letters to him dated [March 15, 1950] and February 1950; and Harry Handy's letter to Don dated February 21, 1950. Dr. Turner has also given his permission to us to use "V for Victory."

The Archives of the University of Illinois at Springfield, where the Handy Writers' collection is housed, gave us permission to quote from Lowney's letters to Harry Handy, April 10, 1951, and Lowney's letters to Mary Ann Jones, September 3, 1951, and April 1, 1952. The Archives made available Mary Ann's unfinished novel, *The Third Time You Killed Me*, and we have summarized it. The Archives also gave us permission to use photographs in the collection.

John Bowers gave us permission to reprint his story and extracts of Lowney's letters to him dated December 16, 1962, and January 7, 1963.

Jon Shirota gave us permission to reproduce his play, The Last Retreat, and to use extracts from Lowney's letters to him dated April 21, 1959, and May 19, 1964.

We were assisted by librarians Barbara Jones and Thomas J. Wood.

Our special thanks to John Bowers, Judith Everson, and J. Michael Lennon for their contributions to this volume; Tinks Howe, who has always helped us; and to Ray Elliott and Vanessa Faurie for editing and publishing this collection of unpublished writings from the Handy Colony.

—H.H., D.S., G.H.